Blessing Love You

Loved ones,
I'm only a whisper away

Mystic Moira

Moira Geoghegan

I dedicate this book
To my family —
Both here on Earth
And in the Spirit World

Design and Print:
Kilkenny People Printing Limited
056 77 63366

Help Lines:
The Samaritans: 1890 609 090
Victim Support: 01 8780870
Campaign Against Bullying: 01 2887976
Alzheimer's Society of Ireland: 065 6823514

Moira Geoghegan (the author)
Multi-gifted Psychic and Trans-Sentient Medium:
Kilkenny, Ireland: 056 7727611

Contents

Acknowledgements

Sincere thanks to all who helped in any way with the production of this book:

Thanks to my family, for their unselfish, loving, continuous, and unflinching support. They have been there for me at every stage of the arduous process of translating creative impulses, spiritual guidance, and inspiration into words that, hopefully, have come close to conveying the messages, ideas, and breathtaking concepts I wish to share with my readers.

To my daughter, Tina Boydell, for her truly inspired and attractive cover design and the beautiful sketches she provided for the book. A picture is worth a thousand words, and Tina is an artist who captures the essence of every theme that catches her eye.

My other three daughters helped in equally important ways to make this volume a reality: Michelle Hayes was my trusty and reliable adviser on all aspects of computer technology.

Saberina took some of the excellent snapshots that appear in the book. Sharon has organised my "field trips" around the country to psychic fairs and other events. She has been a veritable secretary to me, and a great source of strength and support.

Thanks to my cousins, Mary Kelly and Chris Kelly, for procuring photographs. A word of thanks to my son Michael and his wife, Elaine.

I thank my friends, too numerous to mention, who have offered me moral support and good wishes in this publishing venture.

A special thanks to John Fitzgerald, for his time, patience, and dedication: The assistance of a freelance journalist was most welcome. John had previously written about my work in a book entitled *Kilkenny: People Places Faces*.

Thanks to Kilkenny People printers, for a wonderful print layout and overall production.

A sincere mega thank you to the thousands of people, from every corner of this island and from beyond these shores, who have come to me for readings. Many of you call me back to say you have received healing and consolation – I wish the same to all my readers.

Finally, a heartfelt thank you to all those people in the Spirit World who have used me as a channel over the years. It has been a privilege for me to facilitate communication between you and your loved ones on the Earth Plane.

Without you, who now live in the splendour and tranquillity of the Other Side, this book would have remained but a dream and an aspiration. Thanks to you, I can use the power of words to bring your world and ours – closer together.

Preface

For millennia, people have availed of psychic faculties such as Clairvoyance, Clairaudience, and Clairsentience. These are rare gifts. I was born with all three of them.

Less common are the abilities to levitate – rise off the ground, as some saints did when entranced, psycho-kinesis or the ability to move objects without touching them, teleportation, the power to cause physical objects to disappear and re-appear elsewhere, and invisibility.

In the high rocky wastes of the Himalayan Mountains in Tibet, monks have known about these powers – or gifts of the spirit – for centuries. Far removed from the hustle and bustle of evolving modern technology, amid the snowy highlands, they remained in tune with the forces of nature and were receptive to the higher vibrations of the Spirit World.

Though to our Western eyes they might have appeared poor and pitiable, in their humble robes and lack of 'sophistication', they were in fact spiritually far ahead of the so-called civilised world, with its crime, greed, and endless wars.

Today, in our new century, people in Western countries like Ireland are rediscovering the lost truths that the Tibetans of old knew so well: in new age literature, from TV programmes such as Crossing Over With John Edward, at psychic fairs and in the consultation rooms of psychic counsellors like myself, they are learning, or re-learning the great secrets of the ages, and gaining an insight into the real purpose of life on earth.

Rampant atheism and a narrow view of religion are giving way to a new spiritual pluralism that embraces all the religions of the world and the reality of an afterlife.

The average person is familiar with five senses: sight, touch, smell, taste, and hearing. The psychic has a sixth sense that enables him/her to perceive situations beyond the normal range of human faculties. This extra-sensory capability is what sets the psychic apart from the bulk of humanity.

Clairvoyance involves seeing with the "Inner Eye". The Clairvoyant can perceive people and places invisible to normal human vision and located elsewhere in time or space. As well as being able to see everyday physical objects over vast distances, a Clairvoyant can in many cases also perceive spirit people.

The aura that surrounds every human being may also be visible to the Inner Eye, as it is also, I might add, to a special kind of camera that photographs this energy field, thus proving that Clairvoyants were telling the truth down through the centuries when they described the wonderful colours and subtle energies of the aura!

The development of that particular device vindicated the many psychics of the past who were disbelieved and scorned when they spoke of the swirling bands of light they saw around people, animals, and plants.

In the future, hopefully, technological advances will lend credence to all of the other psychic faculties that sceptics and scientists have dismissed in the same way that they once denied the existence of the human aura.

Clairaudience is the ability to hear the voices of spirit people, or occasionally the thoughts of people on the earth plane. A Clairaudient may also pick up other sounds not audible to normal hearing: Angelic music, for example, or what church teaching refers to as the "choirs of angels".

Auric photography has proven the existence of the aura that surrounds every living being: A person's aura reflects his or her level of spiritual development and awareness. Illness can also be diagnosed from analysis of this multi-coloured energy field. This picture shows the author enshrouded by an aura that the photographic agency involved designates as "White, spiritual, enlightened, energy sensitive, transcendent".

It is possible that some people down through the ages who were laughed at for "hearing voices" may have been Clairaudient and really tuned to the Spirit World. If not able to either develop or block out this ability, they may have taken to drink or drugs to kill off the unwanted sixth sense they couldn't cope with.

Clairaudience is not to be confused with the disturbing sounds associated with psychiatric disorders, though it is probable that many gifted psychics in less enlightened eras were locked up, or persecuted due to a misunderstanding of their abilities.

As a medium, being Clairsentient adds to the value of the information and impressions I receive from spirit people during a reading. It enables me to be aware of a spiritual presence by scent and emotion.

When combined with the faculties of seeing and hearing the loved ones who come through, this ability brings home to the sitter the reality of the spirit manifestation.

I become attuned to the spirit person's emotional state. If feelings of grief or sorrow are sent through me, and the loved one sheds a tear of sorrow or happiness for relatives on earth, I not only pick up these emotions - I may also experience the exact same reactions myself – I may feel a little of the pain, the sorrow, the bitterness, or the joy of the spirit person.

All of these remarkable, God given gifts are bestowed on certain people for a purpose: To help and heal our fellow human beings. That is what I hope I have achieved over many years of practise.

M.G.

Introduction

My name is Moira Geoghegan, though I am better known as Mystic Moira. I live just outside the beautiful village of Bennettsbridge in County Kilkenny.

I am told that many people, when they hear my name mentioned, ponder for a second or two and then speak of "the house with all the colours" – a reference to the eye-catching colour scheme that has turned quite a few heads.

Mention of the house is almost inevitably followed by a remark about the large black and amber flag that flies over it – a tribute to the Kilkenny Cats of sporting fame.

Then the conversation tends to shift to what I actually do, and that's when you get to hear a lot of animated comment, observation, on the spot analysis, and a maze-like variety of viewpoints on the subject.

I am a psychic medium, endowed with the power to see and hear beyond the sight and sound frequencies to which the majority of human beings are restricted throughout life on earth. In short, I communicate with people who have "died." I pick up messages from them and relay these to their loved ones on this side of the Great Divide. These are weighty statements. Any claim to be in contact with the unseen worlds is greeted with a mixture of fascination, fear, disbelief, astonishment, or ridicule.

But these initial reactions soon give way to a positive appraisal of what I do.

Scepticism evaporates, fear is replaced by hope and trust, and hostility changes to humble acceptance of what is surely the Best Piece of Good News for struggling, suffering humanity: that death is NOT the end.

I have written this book to communicate the truth that life goes on after death. When I make this emphatic statement I am not offering an opinion. I am not speculating as to what MIGHT be out there in the vast unfathomable universe. I am not engaging in a calculated guess. Nor am I promoting the belief or teaching of any one particular sect or religion-though I respect all of these.

I write, and speak, FROM DIRECT PERSONAL EXPERIENCE. Every day of the week, I see and hear people who are thought of as "dead", whose names are etched on gravestones, who are prayed for at masses, and whose memories are kept alive in the homes of those they left behind.

Every day, I am reminded of the absolute proof that means so much to people who grieve for "lost" friends and relatives. Being Clairvoyant I see those dear loved ones and know they are not lost at all – but living on in a world of breathtaking beauty.

As a Clairaudient, I can hear the voices of people who have retained the personalities, characteristics, likes and dislikes, that they possessed on the earth plane.

They continue to learn and evolve and make friends OVER THERE, picking up from where they left off on earth. And they wish you, their loved ones, to know that they are safe AND HEALED in the Spirit World.

This book is the culmination of many years of work as a psychic medium.

About five years ago, I received advice from the Spirit World to write a book in which I could fluently, effectively and honestly get across the message that death is not to be feared.

It was to be a healing book that would, hopefully, take the sting out of man's greatest fear and replace that perennial sense of dread and foreboding with hope and the knowledge that death is simply a transition – not an earth-shattering, doom-laden calamity.

This was not the first I had heard of the book idea – back in the seventies, a psychic had told me in the Arthur Findlay College in England that I would some day write a book. It was foretold that a man would enter my life and write about me.

This prediction came true. Assisting me in the task of getting the book off the drawing board and onto the bookshelves is John Fitzgerald, author of two publications dealing with his native county. He devoted a chapter to my work as a medium in his *Kilkenny: People Places Faces*.

I waited a while before embarking on this awesome task. I was preoccupied with my work, but eventually, I just had to get around to setting down my message to the world – in writing.

I have now followed through on that advice from advanced, highly evolved spiritual beings. They want you to be aware of their world, and of what awaits you when you cross over from the earth plane.

Many of you will already have met me through the readings. I have had thousands of people come to me over the years – all of them seeking answers to age-old questions about human mortality and survival of death. They come for advice, reassurance, or guidance in relation to past, present or future challenges facing them. But almost every person who makes an appointment to see me hopes to hear from a loved one in the Spirit World. And as a rule, they do not leave disappointed after a reading.

If the person they hope to hear from doesn't come through, another spirit person will most likely have a message for them – perhaps a word or two to let them know that life did not end with that grim funeral day, when the coffin was lowered into the earth.

That was only the mortal remains, discarded like an old or outworn suit of clothes or a car that has seen long service but needed to be replaced. Our loved ones on the Other Side are anxious to put our minds at rest on that score: that all is well in the Spirit World.

I hope to demonstrate in the pages of this book that this other world does indeed exist and that the faith so many people have placed in me is not erroneous or misguided.

Since I started doing readings many moons ago, a daily never-ending stream of visitors has been calling at my home. I get people from all walks of life and from every corner of the land.

No profession, job description, or personality profile is excluded.

A hunger for knowledge of the afterlife transcends all social divides and other distinctions, real or imagined; that separate individuals or groups from each other on earth.

They come too from far beyond these shores. And I receive phone calls from people who want me to know that predictions based on Tarot or Crystal Ball have come true.

The book has chapters dealing with all aspects of my work – but it also focuses on issues that have come up repeatedly during readings.

I open a window into the past – into my own childhood, when the psychic gifts I was born with first began to manifest and come to the notice of those around me.

These rare and precious gifts that enabled me to see "beyond the veil" were with me from the beginning of this present life.

I describe my less than ecstatic experience of "schooling" at the hands of teachers who displayed more skill in the use of sticks and leather straps than in educating children for adult life.

Further trails and tribulations followed hot on the heels of this unhappy phase of my life. After I passed through the gates of the convent school at age twelve, grief, tragedy, struggle, and the pain of loss awaited me.

But throughout those difficult early years, and the challenges that came later, my ability to attune myself to the Higher Dimensions of life remained, and grew stronger.

I am especially indebted to the Arthur Findlay College in England, where I was reminded of how rare and significant were the gifts I had been born with. It was there that I encountered words and definitions that described my psychic abilities: Clairvoyance, Clairsentience, Clairaudience, Trance Mediumship, and so on.

The tutors at the college left me in no doubt as to the importance of my mission in life: To bring to people the comforting and healing truth of life after death; to offer PROOF that life is eternal and that every human being has intrinsic value in the eyes of God, the Higher Spirit.

In the book, I also give my incisive views on religion. I respect all beliefs, but emphasise that no religion, church, or belief system has the right to impose itself on people, or to terrorise or coerce non-believers into accepting its teachings or doctrines.

Though people generally are more open-minded in recent years about all aspects of the paranormal, there are still a lot of sceptics around who swear they will never accept the idea that we survive death. They are entitled to their opinions – but their rejection of what I can actually see and hear any day of the week is a little hard to take. So I have provided some food for thought, with the sceptics in mind. This takes the form of a chapter outlining just a sample of the considerable evidence that has been marshalled over the centuries, but mainly in the past fifty years; which points very clearly in the direction of the afterlife being a reality.

I invite readers to carry out further research of their own in this field. The Internet has thousands of excellent websites specialising in the subject. The evidence for survival of death is truly overwhelming. Having said this, I must again emphasise that I have direct perception of this reality, and do not need to rely on a single shred of evidence or corroborative proof to strengthen my belief in what I know to be true beyond any shadow of a doubt.

I devote a separate chapter to the controversial and topical subject of suicide. It is a tragedy that has reached epidemic proportions in our world. Ireland has not been spared the international upsurge in the numbers of people who take their own lives. The sadness and grief it brings to families are immeasurable. Suicide has been written about extensively, and from many different perspectives. It is seldom out of the news, with a seemingly endless procession of funeral corteges passing before our eyes – on TV screens, along roads, streets, and laneways across the length and breadth of Ireland.

I deal with suicide from the perspective of one who can see what awaits the human spirit on the Other Side.

I bring my many years of experience as a psychic medium to bear on the subject in the hope that my insights, and observations, will help the families of suicide victims – and also help to focus the mind of anyone thinking of committing suicide on the reasons why this is definitely NOT the solution to any of life's problems.

Reincarnation is touched upon – as it must be in any exploration of the mysteries of life and death, and the purpose of life on earth. All of us come to earth with memories of a previous existence.

These memories fade as the child grows on the earth plane and moves further away from his or her point of origin in the Spirit World, from where we all begin our journey into earthly life, and to which we return after death.

Animals have spirits too, so I include a chapter on these friends that keep us company in our earthly lives and with whom we are re-united in the Spirit World.

I deal too with issues that perhaps you might not expect to find in a book on the life and work of a psychic medium: Issues like school and workplace bullying, sexual and physical abuse in the home, betrayal, and the importance of taking responsibility for your actions – the "blame game" being alien to life on the Other Side. I focus on these issues because they have come up in readings and are the issues that urgently need to be addressed, for the sake of justice and harmony on this earth, but also with a view to the long-term effects of dysfunctional human behaviour, bearing in mind that these effects continue to reverberate long after physical death, when we enter the Spirit World.

I hope you will find solace, inspiration, and healing in this book.

CHAPTER 1

Born with the Gift

The bridge at Graiguenamanagh, over the River Barrow.

I WAS born and reared in Graiguenamanagh, County Kilkenny, the town founded by monks in the shadow of the Blackstairs Mountains. Mine was a working-class family. Aside from my parents, I had two brothers and one sister.

I became aware from an early age of my psychic powers. I can remember as a child seeing people around me that were invisible to others. These spirit people – as I later learned they were – could be walking into or out of rooms, or along a street.

At funerals, I saw them: Standing close to mourning loved ones, maybe hugging or embracing them. In graveyards they observed unseen the burial of their own physical bodies.

They tried to comfort grieving relatives, to assure them that death had not obliterated them; that they had just passed to another stage of existence.

Some of these spiritual beings appeared as white forms, others looked more or less as they did during their earthly lives.

In those innocent years, I wondered why nobody else apart from myself was taking any notice of these spirit people at funerals. I got funny looks whenever I drew attention to them. But I was never afraid, even as a child, of what I saw.

We lived in a two-storey house that had a bathroom on the top floor. I remember going upstairs at night and meeting people, who passed me on their way up or down.

They would stand politely aside to make room for me to pass.

The first time I noticed this I asked my mother who else was in the house apart from the family. She gave me strange looks and said "Moira, don't talk like that, you're a peculiar child"!

We used to laugh about these incidents. One day, when I asked her, jokingly, where she got me, my mother said I was dropped on her doorstep whereas the stork had delivered my sister and brothers. Often she shook her head and remarked: "You're definitely a strange one, Moira".

As a child too I had memories of living in a different house, far bigger than our own, and being dressed in a long gown that reached up to my neck and down to my feet. I recalled there was a big collar around my neck in that "other time". I asked my mother about the mysterious house and the unfamiliar garments, and again she looked at me as if I had dropped from the sky.

Such memories of strange or unfamiliar times and places may be flashbacks to a previous existence, as indeed can the reaction of déja-vu; when a feeling comes over you that you have experienced the same emotion, or visited exactly the same location in the past; be it a house, street, or city, or whatever.

I respect and love my family, and I believe that I was born into a specific family situation for a purpose. I believe everything happens for a reason, as part of God's plan for all of us.

A picture that hung in our house in Graiguenamanagh seems, in retrospect, to have pointed towards my later work as a medium. It was a monochrome print of a famous painting by Arthur C. Cooke entitled The Fortune Teller.

As well as indicating the direction my life would take, it also pretty well summed up what has long been the popular attitude to people who can see "beyond the veil" and communicate with the Spirit World:

An elderly mysterious lady sits hunched by an open fire in a shadowy room, holding a crystal ball. She is wrinkled with the wisdom of age, and has a black shawl around her head.

Two children approach her hesitantly, perhaps in the hope of gaining knowledge of the future, or then again, they could have entered her humble abode out of idle curiosity, having heard the usual gossip and ill-informed speculations about one who has access to the unseen worlds:

Arthur C. Cooke's "The Fortune Teller": It hung on the wall of the Geoghegan family home in Graiguenamanagh for generations and seemed to point the way to Moira's future as a psychic medium.

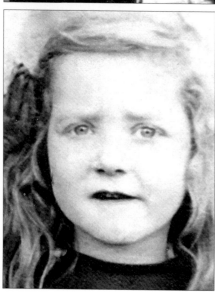

In the past, anyone who had a psychic gift ran the risk of incurring, not just ridicule and misunderstanding, but the wrath of organised religion. The painting is open to many interpretations. On the wall over the fireplace hangs a sprig of heather for good luck.

The picture was always in my parents' house. Today, it hangs proudly in the consultation room of my home in Bennettsbridge. The enigmatic lady in the picture and her young visitors could be said to represent the work I do.

And its presence in the old homestead could have had a purpose: To convey the message to me that knowledge of other dimensions would play a crucial part in the future that lay, as yet undiscovered, before me.

Top: Tom and John Purcell, the author's maternal uncles.

Middle: Moira with her mother, at home in Graiguenamanagh.

Bottom: Psychic from birth: Moira, aged 8.

Going back to my childhood, I am very conscious of the fact that children are aware of the psychic world. Uninhibited by pre-conceived notions and age-old prejudices, they are often more open to the Greater Reality than adults tend to be.

When they refer to invisible playmates, they may be telling the truth, and not merely "imagining things", as parents assure them is the case.

Children are gifted and privileged in this respect- it is their families who make them afraid, who tell them not to be talking nonsense, or to "grow up". Due to this conditioning, they gradually lose their sensitivity to the wonderful world of the spirit.

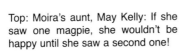

Top: Moira's aunt, May Kelly: If she saw one magpie, she wouldn't be happy until she saw a second one!

Bottom: Tina Boydell, the author's daughter, who designed the book cover.

As children, ALL OF US are more attuned to the psychic realms until adults make us afraid, or, as they see it, "knock sense into us".

This is sad, because it deprives so many people of the ability to perceive other dimensions that are part of God's creation.

I was fortunate, in that I retained and developed my psychic powers. Instead of losing my gift, as I grew older, like other children, my powers became stronger.

On a humorous note, I remember how my mother had absolutely no hesitation about visiting our local graveyard in pitch darkness! When her sister, my aunt May in Castlemorris came to our home, she, my mother, and I would sometimes take a little tour of the cemetery.

With the aid of a torch, they loved to look up information on the people whose bodies were interred. It was a kind of leisure pursuit that absorbed and fascinated them.

They could spend hours looking at the names on the headstones and chatting about who this person and that person were... and who the relatives might be.

Re-visiting the town of her childhood: The author at the beautiful quayside in Graiguenamanagh, Co. Kilkenny.

Picture: Saberina

They pored over and evaluated the inscriptions, debating with themselves about the lives and times of the real people behind the inscribed names and dates on the cold moss coated slabs of stone.

Anyway, one night we were moving about the graveyard without a care in the world when a man happened to pass by on the road outside. He was a local character who used to whistle and sing under the streetlights of Graiguenamanagh.

All he saw in the graveyard was the light of the torch moving among the graves and headstones. Terrified out of his wits, he emitted an unmerciful screech and took to his heels, hightailing it back into town. He believed he had seen a ghostly form hovering about and decided not to hang around.

My mother had the right idea: Though she often chided me on my psychic ability, she had no fear of the dead herself. Calling to the graveyard at night was no more frightening or off-putting for her than a daytime visit.

This was an enlightened attitude-because the spirits of the dead pose no threat to us: It's the ones down here that we need to watch!

My mother used to tell that story over and over again and laugh at it. My aunt May had her own superstitions, as most people had in those days. If she saw a magpie on the road, she would have no peace of mind until she saw another one. It was deemed unlucky to spot one magpie.

CHAPTER 2

Learning the Hard Way

AT SCHOOL, I learned to keep quiet about what I saw. I could "read the cards", though I didn't use these at school. I found I could divine the future, see into the mists of time and foretell events in the lives of people, young and old; that I met.

Though my psychic powers didn't require the cards, I found that these served as a focus, and, just as importantly, people seemed happier when the cards were there as it added to the mystique of a reading for them.

Not that I had much time to concentrate on spiritual matters at school. It wasn't exactly a fun-filled phase of my life. It was closer to being a nightmare. I am self-taught, not by choice as much as by necessity. The school I attended up to the age of 12 was a disaster from an educational point of view. I can honestly say that I left it without having learned anything much of value.

The ironically named Convent of Mercy in Graiguenamanagh was better at dishing out brutality and punishment than it was at preparing children for adult life.

There was little mercy shown by the veiled sisters who wielded the dreaded wooden "pointers" and leather straps. According to an old proverb, your school days were supposed to be the happiest days of your life. Mine certainly weren't. The nuns at the Convent of Mercy ran their school with an iron fist.

The Convent of Mercy, Graignamanagh, where nuns ruled with an iron fist.

If they had been just strict disciplinarians, it would have been harsh enough, and difficult for us pupils to endure, but they were more than that. Some of them brought cruelty to a fine art in the classroom.

While purporting to be servants of God and devoted to Christianity, they exhibited a callous disregard for the humane principles of tolerance and compassion that inspire the Christian belief.

They picked on some of us more than others. A kind of caste system prevailed in the school. The nuns concentrated on teaching pupils from well-to-do families, like the daughters of shopkeepers, doctors, and bank managers.

My own father – Simon Geoghegan – was a farm labourer. He was an honest man who worked hard to support his family. He had to walk six miles to punch in a strenuous day's labour on the farm and return on foot to the house.

It might be midnight before he got back. I remember one day my brother needed money for something and decided to go where my father worked to see if the farmer would hand over the wages, as it would be late when the money arrived home.

Moira, with her sister Kathleen, who has made her confirmation. Kathleen also felt the wrath of the nuns.

The old farmer looked him up and down and scowled: "He hasn't it earned yet, boy". There were few soft jobs or cushy careers at that time.

I found that having working class parents was a disadvantage in the school. It seemed that farm labouring wasn't "kosher" with the holy nuns. I was one of about ten pupils in my class who were literally ignored by the teachers.

We were relegated to the back of the classroom. Our written compositions or other exercises, however long or hard we worked on them were frowned upon and seldom checked or corrected.

The nuns carried on as if we didn't exist. If we raised our hands to answer questions during history or religion classes, the teachers ignored us. The attitude seemed to be: "how dare we presume to know anything". We were just filling up spaces in the classroom. I loved history. I loved hearing or reading about the great personalities and events of the past that shaped our world.

Likewise, all the children had their favourite subjects. So it hurt that the nuns ignored me, meeting my efforts and trusting curiosity with a look that could have cut me in half.

There was no serious effort to teach us, just to keep us in our place, under control, until the bell rang to sound the ending of another pointless day in class.

Though the nuns didn't bother to educate our little group of less well off pupils, they showed an uncommonly keen interest in any of us who turned up late, even by a minute or two, for school.

The country children had to walk up to three miles to school each morning in all kinds of weather. Through

Unhappy school days: Moira sets off for another "lesson" from the women in black.

hail, rain, or snow, they had to trek with their bags or cases to the austere convent building. In winter, they'd arrive soaked to the skin, or shivering with the cold.

Instead of showing concern for them, the nun on duty would look at the clock and remind them that they had missed the 10 o'clock roll call. The children knew what that meant: punishment!

The pointer came out, and the children were ordered to line up. They were subjected to a ferocious bout of slapping. This practise always struck me as one of the great anomalies in the school: Since we country girls never learned anything anyway, what was the

Kathleen in later years.

point of slapping us for the "offence" of not turning up on time?

Having long hair was another disadvantage for a pupil at the Convent of Mercy.

I had long hair and the nuns hated it. Whenever a nun was having a bad day, I dreaded to see her moving in my direction. She'd grab me by the hair and hop my head off the desk.

This happened to many girls. It was so commonplace that we just looked upon it as part of the classroom routine.

Of course, a pupil did not need to have long hair to hear and feel the painful thud of her head banging on the wooden desktop. If there weren't a curl or a tress to grapple, your head would still thump the hard surface with the aid of a hearty push from an "educator".

The only bit of fun we had was when the mothers of pupils who had been ill-treated came in to confront the nuns. We shed tears of laughter as we watched the mothers chase the nuns around the schoolyard and rip the veils off their heads. Some of our tormentors got badly mauled by those angry women.

I can understand only too well why the mothers resorted to such extreme measures: My sister Kathleen went to the technical school in Graiguenamanagh. One night, my mother noticed that she was unable to turn on either of her sides in the bed and appeared in be in pain.

She removed Kathleen's clothing and was stunned at the sight of her: Her two arms were black and blue from bruising. She had been severely beaten by teachers at the Tech.

My brother attended the boy's school. He too experienced the downside of the so-called "education system". He left school practically illiterate due to the failure of the male teachers to teach him.

There was a strong emphasis on corporal punishment in his school – to put it mildly – but also a total disregard for the progress of certain pupils, as in the convent school I attended.

Most days, he was ordered to leave the room and stand outside in the yard, or to cut slappers from tree branches to be used in the classrooms.

He was very often the first pupil to get beaten with them. His school experience was both unhappy and without value, as he learned almost nothing in the course of his time there.

As I say, I had to educate myself after leaving school because of the crazy situation that pertained in the convent. In retrospect, though I resent very much how the nuns behaved, I can understand the plight many of them found themselves in.

At that time, girls were often coerced into entering convents. Families considered it a badge of honour to have a daughter donning the veil and becoming, as they saw it, a servant of God by taking the vow of celibacy that went with being a nun.

Any girl who became a nun was deemed by our profoundly Catholic society to have been personally called by God, and her religious vocation had to be respected.

Unfortunately, all too many of these women entered convents, not in response to a divine entreaty, but simply to appease their families.

Any other childhood or youthful ambitions they may have nurtured, or indeed any notions of marrying, had to be abandoned or suppressed to make way for their enforced "vocations".

Small wonder that these nuns – unwilling participants in Ireland's religious establishment – vented their frustrations on the children they were supposed to educate.

In a way, they were as much victims of the religious fundamentalism and man-made church laws prevalent at the time as the pupils they taught – or failed to teach.

Not all the nuns in Graiguenamanagh were nasty. I remember one low sized nun who was kind to us and always had a pleasant smile. We liked to walk alongside her in the schoolyard and listen to her words of wisdom. And she never had that cruel or sadistic look on her face like the others.

CHAPTER 3

The Lady in White

MY FIRST job after leaving school was at Jerves Street hospital in Dublin. Every night when I came down from duty I went into the mortuary to say a prayer.

None of the other staff members or workers would come in with me. I remember one night I went in and noticed a young girl there amid the corpses. Her body was still warm. I knelt down beside her and prayed. Suddenly, I felt a hand touch my head. The girl's arm had slipped and fallen against me.

I then heard her spirit voice: "I'm happy, I'm at peace now", she said. I then realised that she was in spirit. This was my first such encounter in the mortuary. I told her I was glad she was at peace.

I returned to my dormitory and went to bed. From that night onwards, I began to see spirits in the hospital wards. They acknowledged me with friendly smiles. There was never a trace of hostility or negative feeling towards me.

They were of all ages-many of them appeared to be waiting for their loved ones to collect their mortal bodies for burial. I learned not to speak about what I saw there – I had to be tactful – though I continued to visit the mortuary.

The staff never ceased to be amazed that I had no fear of what for them was a bleak and depressing section of the building that they wished to avoid.

Moira with Nurse Fitzgerald, in the hosptial at Merrion, Dublin.

I tried to explain that there was nothing there to be feared, that the spirit beings posed no threat to anybody. The significance of the gift I had became increasingly evident to me.

Later, I took the boat to England and got married over there. I had some interesting experiences in a few of the old houses. I had a memorable encounter in the flat where I lived. One night, I sensed a lot of psychic activity around me. I heard a female voice that had a gentle, beautiful resonance to it. "Moira", the voice intoned softly.

Seeing nobody, I thought at first it might have been an elderly relative who had been in the flat earlier – but she had just gone out for a social evening with two other relations of mine.

I was making sandwiches for the three of them, awaiting their return, and also keeping an eye on the children who had gone to bed. I was baffled as to where the voice had come from.

Then the lady spoke again: "I am lost", she said, "I can't find my husband, can you find him for me?" Still unsure of where the voice originated, I entered the children's bedroom, thinking that perhaps the woman had frightened them.

But they were sleeping soundly. I heard the voice again: "Don't worry, I've been looking after them", it assured me. It dawned on me that I was listening to a spirit voice.

The lady spoke once more, telling me who she was and that she had lost her husband in foreign lands in a war situation. I did what I could, arranging for the house to be blessed.

A few evenings later, the lady and her husband appeared to me in the house. They were holding hands. She had good news: "I found him", she revealed, "We've found each other". The man was wearing an army summer uniform.

He had a row of medals on his jacket. I was happy for this couple. Their search was over and they had been joyously re-united in spirit. I never saw or heard from them after that.

I can recall other paranormal experiences in the same flat – I had to warn a relative when she visited the house that strange or unnerving things might occur and that she ought not to be frightened or nervous if the lights suddenly went on and off or if any other manifestations occurred during her presence in the building.

In particular, I was aware of a spirit lady who dropped into the flat occasionally. Instead of simply walking through the door or walls to enter the flat, as she could easily have done, this lady preferred to open and shut the door in the normal way, as she would have been used to while in her earthly body.

I should explain that there was a bolt on the sitting room door, as this doorway opened on to a stairs leading from our top floor flat. The bolt had to fastened whenever the two children were playing in the room to prevent them from falling down the stairs.

One evening, a relative of mine was relaxing in the sitting room, smoking a cigarette, when she heard a creaking noise. It came from the door. To her horror and disbelief, the bolt had slid open on the door by itself.

The door opened gently and closed again, seemingly by itself. The spirit lady had been in the room and was just leaving.

My relative went white with fear. Her hands shaking, she took a tentative pull on the cigarette and said: "Moira, would you mind walking me down the stairs to the front door". I had never seen so much fear in a person's face.

I tried to calm her, and explain that there was nothing to worry about. She wondered, as other relatives did, why I stayed in the house at all, with those spiritual manifestations.

They looked at me as if I was off my head when I told them I had no fear of such things, and that the comings and goings of spirit people in the house was quite natural. The visiting spirit lady spoke to me frequently. She always had a friendly disposition.

From then onwards, my powers became more enhanced. Messages from the Spirit World came "quick and heavy". When walking down a street, for example, I could look at complete strangers and know which of them were due to depart the earthly plane in the near future.

I knew that a person's earthly life span was nearing its end even in cases when he or she felt perfectly healthy and not aware of any illness.

My spirit guides told me that my job here on earth was two-fold: to heal the pain of bereavement – and to relay messages from loved ones on the Other Side. This was my mission or purpose in life.

CHAPTER 4

Sadness and Joy

I T HAS been said, and written, that people endowed with the gift of psychic mediumship tend to have tough lives and great hardship, partly because they need to understand the challenges of life firsthand.

This then confers an important advantage when they seek to help, guide, or enlighten their fellow human beings who come to them with every conceivable problem or crisis imaginable.

I have known multiple tragedy and heartache in my life. I have been at the coalface of real pain, grief, and sorrow. Thank God, I am not only still around to tell the tale, but indeed in a stronger position to help others who are struggling in one way or another.

Suffering refines the soul, though it can either make or break any human being. Luckily, I have found the strength to gain from it.

The early years were full of challenge. I was just four months pregnant with my fifth child when news came through that Michael, my brother, had been murdered in London.

Three weeks later, I was admitted to hospital. I was very ill and seemed to be losing the child. The doctors kept telling me: "Moira, we'll save you, but baby will go".

I went into labour during Christmas week. The sister came to me and suggested that I ask Michael to help. I hadn't thought about

Michael Geoghegan, Moira's brother ... he appeared to her in hospital shortly after departing the Earth Plane.

that. So I asked Michael to pray for God to help me through my ordeal, and to keep me safe to rear my family.

Almost immediately, a small cloud formed over me in the labour ward. Gradually, it filled the space above me and Michael's face appeared in it.

He looked exactly as he did as a young man, full of vibrant youth and vigour, and wearing a broad, cheery smile.

I knew then that everything would be okay. I asked Michael if a priest had attended to him at his hour of death. He confirmed that a priest was there. I mentioned this to him because my mother, being a strong Catholic, was anxious about Michael receiving the Last Rites.

She had been devastated by his death and was relieved to learn that a priest had given him the Final Blessing. She knew then that Michael was in Heaven.

DEATH OF A CHILD - BIRTH OF AN ANGEL

Every mother knows the unfathomable grief and sense of irreplaceable loss occasioned by the death of a child. I can empathise with such loss. I have known the pain and the grief.

But also, because I am psychic and a medium, I have the consolation of knowing for certain that what we perceive as a loss is viewed from a different perspective in the Spirit World. The baby we grieve for down here is received by loving carers and relatives when this most innocent of loved ones is taken from us.

I lost a son at almost nine months – a full term baby. His lungs were not developed. I was very ill with that child. I asked for help on that occasion too, and all my loved ones gathered around. I saw my Guardian Angel and my spirit guide in the ward.

They explained who they were and told me I would be fine.

Patrick-Joseph was my third child. I had two children before him. With my first two children, I had all the baby clothes bought before the birth, but when carrying Patrick Joseph, I had bought only one or two basic items of clothing.

I knew, somehow, that he was not going to live on the earthly plane so I had not bought or gathered together the necessary clothing.

All through that pregnancy the nurses told me that it was a big baby and that everything would be okay. But Patrick Joseph passed to the Spirit World.

I had a similar feeling when carrying what would have been my fifth child, a baby girl. I hadn't collected the clothes together either in her case as the spirits had told me she wouldn't survive. She was not for this world.

I had two more children after that and from the moment I knew of the pregnancies I went out and bought the clothes, the prams, and everything else for these babies. I was sure that all would be well for them. The babies who died went to the Spirit World, as I was promised they would. My spiritual guides had equally assured me that I would live on those two occasions.

I have seen my dear spirit children, Patrick and Mary, on many occasions. I see them because I am Clairvoyant, but let me assure anyone reading this who has lost a child, whether through miscarriage, Sudden Cot Death Syndrome, illness, or termination, that your loved one is safe and healed in the Spirit World.

Though we think of our dear one's departure from the earth plane as a loss, and a tragedy, he or she is at peace in a world that far surpasses this planet of ours in beauty and true love, the unselfish kind of love that embraces all human beings and is not rationed or confined by ignorance or prejudice.

I balance my loss with the knowledge that Patrick and Mary are safe and well on a happier plane of existence. Equally, I love and treasure my five children on the earth plane: Tina, Sharon, Michelle, Saberina, and Michael.

They have been a tower of strength and support to me through good times and bad. The hardship I have endured at various junctures in my life has been more than offset by the love, kindness, and loyalty they have shown me.

I value their support, and I am also aware of my spirit children growing to maturity in the Spirit World.

So... Do not think of your child as having "died", for death is not ever what it seems to the uninitiated. Death to the earth plane is birth to a greater life. Your babies are angels in the life beyond and you will meet them again. That, believe me, is a prospect to look forward to!

Outside Moira's mother's home in Graiguenamanagh.

CHAPTER 5

A College for Psychics

W HEN I lived at Woodgreen in London, I got to hear of a centre that specialised in helping people to develop their mediumship. This was the Arthur Findlay College in Stansted, England. I decided to try it out. The college was a revelation.

I fell in love with it from my first glimpse of its stately structure and outline against a picturesque natural backdrop. It is set in the midst of landscaped Victorian parkland, close to a lake that has wooed the romantic and artistically minded for centuries.

The college is at Stansted Hall, which was converted and transformed into a centre for psychic and spiritual development. Arthur Findlay, a distinguished pioneer in the field of psychic research and investigation, founded the college. Its aim, now as in the past, is to promote and advance the study of psychic science and spiritualism.

I enrolled for a one-week course at the college. It was quite intensive, but a most enriching and enjoyable experience. Each day, you attended classes and underwent training from 10 am to 9.30 pm, with only a break for lunch in between. But the work and effort involved was well worthwhile.

Here was a place where the powers I had been born with; that came naturally to me; were spoken about freely, and where people were actively encouraged to fine-tune what psychic skills they had, or to nurture and develop such abilities "from scratch", depending on the level of psychic endowment in the case of each student.

Students were broken up into small groups seated around tables. Tutors took them through all the stages of establishing contact with the Spirit World.

These sessions involved meditation, reflection, and painstakingly patient analysis of the various attempts by aspiring mediums to pick up impressions and messages from the Other Side.

I remember one day, large numbers of us were seated in the vast assembly hall, and the tutor was on a stage at the top of the hall. He asked us all to close our eyes and make our minds blank to facilitate a psychic experience.

Total silence descended over the hall. But after a minute or two, I heard the sound of footsteps. I couldn't resist opening my eyes.

I saw a spirit person walking at ease around the building. Some of the others heard the footsteps too, though I imagine not too many actually saw the spirit – I was combining Clairvoyance (seeing) and Clairaudience (hearing), though it was later that I learned the meanings of these terms describing psychic faculties.

Another day, I saw a spirit person touring the hall, with a pen and notebook in one of his hands.

He halted momentarily beside various students, apparently noting observations on each person, before moving to the next one, as if he were performing some form of "assessment" on the students!

The course included explanations of the various powers and abilities, spanning the entire psychic spectrum. By the end of the week, the tutors had assessed all of us. Then came the moment of truth for the students.

They were told if they had psychic potential or not, and which talents should be developed. Each student learned of his strengths and weaknesses. This final day of the course was fraught with tension for some: The tutors had to convey bad news to those who showed little or no promise. This could be a bitter blow to anyone with high ambitions but who lacked psychic potential.

Others found they had prospective ability in one area, perhaps in the field of crystal gazing or tarot reading, but not as mediums, and so on.

When my turn came and the tutor approached me, I was unsure what to expect. She was, it turned out, deeply impressed at what I had demonstrated of my abilities during the week. "Moira", she advised, "you are especially gifted across a whole range of abilities: You are clairvoyant, clairaudient, and clairsentient".

This was news to me. I was aware of a gift, but I had never put names or labels on what I did.

She went on to say that I had a mission in life, to help people back in Ireland through my powers as a medium, to bring hope and consolation to the countless bereaved families by demonstrating to them that we survive bodily death and live on in the Spirit World.

As it happened, my weeklong stay at the college proved to be the first of many visits to this spiritual centre of learning. I was asked to return and teach newcomers to the field of psychic phenomena.

I soon found myself helping students with their psychic development. Generally, these hadn't been born with the gift and were therefore not natural mediums. They would have to devote a lot of time and practise to become more attuned to the spiritual realms.

My work with aspiring mediums yielded some interesting moments. One 19-year old student was very committed to developing his dormant spiritual power. After a few minutes sitting opposite me at a table, he began tentatively to describe a dog he saw or sensed around me. "It's like a fox", he opined.

In fact, I had lost a dog called "Foxy" some time before, so this rather impressed me. At other tables, I helped, nudged, and guided students towards fuller expression of their abilities.

During a reading I did for a young German woman, her father came through quite strongly. I went into a deep trance and this elderly man from the Spirit World took me over almost completely. I saw through his eyes, as it were. I felt many years older and a sensation of moving slowly ... in accordance with the rigours of advanced age.

The spirit took me up a stairway. I ascended the steps laboriously. Half way to the top, I was stopped in my tracks by a beautiful painting on a wall facing me. Further up, I came to an attic.

The spirit released me from his influence and I described for his daughter what I had seen. She was ecstatic: At the mention of a painting, she explained that he had been an artist. He had lived in the loft of the house.

During another deep trance, I was taken-or guided-through a garden that could truly be described as "out of this world". Multihued flowers abounded, flecked with colours unknown to our earthly spectrum. Lovely hedges meandered through this vision of Paradise. The atmosphere was that of a bright, calm, tranquil summer's day.

A feeling of peace and sweet harmony pervaded the scene. Down a little path I walked, and ahead of me appeared an angelic lady accompanied by a child.

This gentle, radiant woman told me the child was one of my own that had passed to the spirit world. The feeling of utter joy and contentment was such that I would gladly have remained in that garden. I didn't want to come back!

As I said, I discovered at the college that the multiple psychic gifts that I had been born with had been given different names for convenience by researchers into the paranormal. The ability to see spirit beings or the auras that surround every person is called clairvoyance.

Clairaudience has to do with hearing spirit voices, or the unspoken thoughts of people. Clairsentience involves being aware of the presence of spirit beings or phenomena by sensing them, perhaps by smelling a distinctive perfume, powder, or brand of tobacco they used on earth.

At the college, I learned of the fascinating history of spiritualism in Britain and other parts of the world. On the walls were pictures and paintings that honoured mediums of the past. I noticed that some of these had employed techniques and practises in their work that I was unfamiliar with at that point:

One picture showed a medium in a trance, with a strange vapoury whitish substance seemingly emanating from her mouth and forming itself into what resembled a human form.

This, I learned, was ectoplasm, an ethereal force that some mediums can generate and which is then drawn upon by spirit people and utilized to make their presence felt in a sèance room.

Ectoplasm can in certain cases be used to create a temporary voice box – or replica of human vocal chords –, enabling a spirit to speak directly with those present at the sèance. Hundreds of such communications have been recorded and provide some of the best evidence for life after death.

Other photographs at the college depicted the use of trumpets at sèances. Spirit voices could apparently be heard through these, and the instruments also moved about by themselves in certain situations.

The work of "Physical mediums", in whose presence spirits cause furniture to move and noises or rappings to be heard, differs from mental mediumship, in which the psychic hears the spirit messages and passes these on to the sitter.

Of immense interest too were the spirit photographs displayed at the college. Since the invention of photography, there have been numerous instances of spirit people, or forms resembling departed loved ones, appearing on film.

Examples of such snapshots fascinated me when I saw them at Arthur Findlay's. They offered further evidence to the cynics and sceptics of this world that the human personality survives death.

In later years, I had an exhilarating firsthand experience of this phenomenon: A picture of myself showed vapoury forms of the kind associated with spirit photography. A picture of my mother contains quite a few spirit manifestations.

She is sitting, relaxed, in an armchair, oblivious to the presence of visitations from the Other Side.

In another striking photograph, one featuring my grandson, I could identify the faces of several deceased family members on the door of the room in which it was snapped. In addition to these, a peculiar light or glow seems to emanate from both sides of the same door.

I refer the reader to these pictures, which I include in the book.

One day, while in the assembly hall of the college, I was told by a psychic medium that a man would enter my life in the future and would write about me, and that I would embark on the task of writing a book myself. I believe this man has indeed arrived in my life.

He is John Fitzgerald, who I know will be famous in his own right. After hearing about my work, he came to visit me in the summer of 2002. At a later date, he wrote a chapter about my life and work as a medium in a book dealing with people and places in County Kilkenny.

He has tried to foster an awareness and better understanding of the spiritual side of life and to break down the barrier between earth and the spirit realms, bringing the two worlds closer together. I believe he was 'sent' to help me with advice and support in writing my book.

The college tutors suggested I do what is termed platform work in Ireland, meaning public demonstrations of mediumship. But I found that Irish attitudes to the subject differed from those I had encountered across the water.

Private sittings were more in tune with the way Irish people perceived the whole idea of communication between the spirit and physical worlds. Even today, I still get a lot of people who would be mortified if their friends or families knew they were coming for readings. If they see a second car in the yard when they arrive, they drive away and return later. I respect their right to privacy, but I look forward to a day when Irish people generally approach matters of the spirit with a greater openness.

Attitudes have certainly improved in recent years. Psychic fairs, and TV programmes on the paranormal, have helped to create a deeper awareness and appreciation of the truth concerning life after death.

Though I do readings privately, the sheer numbers of bookings I get says something about the level of interest in life beyond the physical plane and about the deep-seated need people have to hear from their departed loved ones.

People who would describe themselves as born sceptics come to me. Despite their outward cynicism towards what I do, they begin to relent a little as the reading progresses.

Once messages come through for them, doubts fade and they sit up and take notice of these "Postcards from Heaven", as a poet once dubbed spirit communications. The evidence is there before them, clear and incontestable.

Others pretend to friends, family, and workmates that they think nothing of "that old nonsense" and speak disparagingly of the very idea that life goes on after death.

But this is often just a protective façade, a smokescreen to hide their sincere inner belief, or suspicion, that this world is but a prelude to a higher level of existence.

The teachings of organised religion and the attitudes of narrow scientific institutions have pushed their beliefs "underground", though such people may have at least one close confidante to whom they reveal their true feelings and opinions on the matter.

Centuries of propaganda and ignorance of the spiritual realms have fostered this climate of denial and prevarication.

But thankfully that situation is now changing, however slowly, and giving way to a new dawn of spiritual awareness and understanding, like a flower opening up to the rays of an Indian summer.

There is a hunger for knowledge, and proof, of an afterlife. The various churches and religions preach about life after death, but their followers, however strong their faith might be, are anxious to receive some definite confirmation, some scrap of evidence, that will demonstrate to them conclusively that the drama acted out in the graveyards of this world does not represent life's Final Curtain.

Every family is affected by grief, by the loss of loved ones, and a medium may offer the best hope of setting their minds at rest.

Whether the long awaited for proof of survival comes in a lecture hall or hotel conference centre, where mediums do platform work, or in the calm privacy of my consultation room, the effect is similar:

Relief and happiness for the grieving person who now knows the truth: that death is a mere transition from a world of woe to a place of peace and joy.

The Arthur Findlay College at Stansted, England, where Moira has given tutorials in psychic development.

CHAPTER 6

Death: Transition to a New and Happier Life ...

THE subject of death is one that many people wish to avoid. It is a taboo that modern man pushes to the back of his mind, a reality that seems too grim and dreadful to contemplate.

Vast amounts of money and exhaustive medical research have been devoted to finding ways of deferring death for as long as possible.

Ever more ingenious technology is being devised to prolong earthly life and postpone the moment that materialistic science views with cold horror, and that believers in the various forms of religion, whatever their concept of the afterlife, regard with almost equal misgiving and insecurity.

The twin teachings or beliefs of traditional science and organised religion, though contradictory, combine to induce a terror of death:

Science would have us believe that death involves the total extinction of the human being, that we are nothing but animated heaps of flesh, blood, skin, and bones that wither ... and disappear into the earth ... after the heart stops and the brain shuts down.

That's one extreme view that I know to be utterly false. But the other extreme position, the one offered by organised religion, can also be off the mark.

Religions state that, yes, there is life after death, but that God is a vengeful master who dispatches anyone who doesn't measure up to his expectations to Hell, to burn for all eternity without any possibility of "parole" or a second chance.

From my firsthand psychic knowledge of the Spirit World, I can definitely state that neither extreme bears any relation to the TRUTH. Death is not the end, as the atheist or hard-bitten scientist or sceptic will tell you.

But neither is it followed by the kind of horror tale scenario described by those zealous preachers who used to bang the pulpits and put the fear of God into people.

EXTREME VIEW OF AFTERLIFE UNFOUNDED

On the ceiling of the Sistine Chapel in the Vatican can be seen Michelangelo's famous painting The Last Judgement. The work depicts a frightening vision of the afterlife that has inspired-and terrorised-so many generations of people in the western world, including Ireland.

Angels in the painting appear as grim bearers of justice, fighting or struggling with the "damned" and helping to cast them into Hell. There is no mercy shown to anyone who has fallen by the wayside in life and no "second chance" in this version of what happens after death.

A grief-stricken woman raises her hands and arms in a plea for clemency-but none is forthcoming. A man seems to have just realised that his change of heart has come too late-a demon catches hold of him. Another poor fellow is falling into the flames.

In this depiction of the afterlife, the righteous – those who happened to die at the right time, meaning AFTER repenting and begging forgiveness, go UP while the sinners who died before they could cleanse their souls go DOWN to the abode of the cloven hoofed Devil to burn forever.

If such utterly false and nightmarish images were confined to paintings and Hollywood horror movies, they might not be so bad.

Unfortunately, these dubious and unfounded impressions of what happens to us after death have been used to frighten the living daylights out of devout Christians for centuries.

From my own direct perception of the Spirit World I know this negative and mind-boggling version of our immortal destiny is pure invention and fabrication. You have nothing to fear in leaving your physical body at the point of death.

God is compassionate and just. God is the Higher Spirit who looks after all of us, a creator to be loved rather than feared. He is not a dictator up in the clouds waiting to wreak havoc on people who fall by the wayside in life.

It was the height of nonsense-as already stated- for some of the priests of old to condemn or frighten people who sought happiness and contentment through second relationships when their marriages failed.

Far from "sinning", or offending God, these people had to pick up the pieces after the sad conclusion of what promised to be a life-long loving commitment.

There will be no punishment for this common sense approach on the Other Side, so please ... don't fear death on account of all that judgemental and scary sermonizing that mass-goers had to put up with in the bad old days.

TO BE WELCOMED ... NOT FEARED

Death is no more to be feared than sleep. Indeed, sleep has often been referred to as "the little death" because it rounds off each day and precedes the arrival of another bright new dawn.

Though the illness or fatal event that brings about the process may be painful, the transition from the earth plane to the Other Side is painless and indeed a wonderfully liberating experience. This is why people who have had "near death" encounters never forget the joy and beauty of what they have seen.

These patients in many parts of the world have been medically revived in hospital after being declared clinically dead. They temporarily leave their bodies and find that all pain has vanished, no matter how severe the accident or illness might have been.

Looking down at their physical bodies, they feel a sense of detachment and a great reluctance to return to the sick, injured, or pain-racked shell lying in the bed below them.

Apart from the sensation of moving outside the body, many of them are blessed with an insight, however brief or ephemeral, of another dimension beyond the physical.

Upon awakening, they have described their fleeting glimpses of a joyous and exhilarating world that awaits all of us.

They speak of meeting deceased family members or old friends, who receive them with love, understanding, and conviviality – but advise them that their time on earth has not yet ended, and that they must return to their physical bodies to complete their allotted span on earth.

I have had many out of body experiences. During a difficult birth, I found myself floating above my sleeping, pain-racked body that lay in a hospital bed.

I hovered unseen in the room, wondering what the doctors and nurses were fussing about when I felt great, with my bird's eye view of the proceedings in the maternity ward.

Apart from the medical staff, I became aware of other presences around me: I felt the love and concern of spirit beings ... family members I had lost were there.

When I saw and heard them, I wanted to leave with these dear friends and relatives. Wouldn't anyone feel the same? The prospect of entering into a beautiful new world of spirit was enticing and almost irresistible. But this option was not open to me.

They advised me that my life mission was not yet complete. There was much yet to be accomplished on earth. I had to rear my children, and other tasks or challenges lay ahead. My allotted life span had far from run its course. So I returned to my body and regained physical consciousness.

I should mention here that none of us crosses over to the Spirit World until our appointed time. Our lives are mapped for us from birth, though free will ensures that nothing is written in stone, so we may diverge here and there along life's journey.

You hear of people who survive battles or wars when comrades fall around them. They seem to have "charmed lives", as the saying goes, but in fact they are being watched over and shielded from premature exiting of the physical plane.

So, seemingly against all the odds, they come through the flames of battle, or survive earth-shattering events to soldier on to the end of life's journey. They still had tasks to perform and lessons to learn ... so they were spared.

For the same reason, anyone not ready to pass over will survive even the most hazardous operation and pull through because of their "unfinished business" on earth and the hurdles they still must face before the final whistle blows for them.

Many people who have undergone so-called "near death experiences" recall being advised by a radiant spirit being that they cannot yet cross the Great Divide or bridge from the earth plane to the Other Side: As in my own case, they accept, though often reluctantly, that they must complete life's journey before passing over.

Though we grieve and lament for the dead, we should remember that they have not been obliterated or destroyed. They have just cast off an earthly shell like we discard an old jacket or worn out suit of clothes. What they leave behind is not a person, but simply an abandoned "vehicle" that has served its purpose.

Monks and other holy people concerned with the transition of our spirits from the earth plane to the Spirit World have consulted the Tibetan Book of the Dead, an immortal classic on the Eastern World, for centuries. It tells how a trained clairvoyant lama will sit by the dying person and carry on a conversation by telepathy with the departing spirit, offering guidance on the stages of her/her progress to the higher levels of being.

Not that such guidance from this side of the Great Divide is necessary for a spirit that has broken free from the physical body. Our loved ones will be there for us when the time comes.

The ancient Egyptians also resorted to a book of wisdom dealing with the afterlife state. Their beliefs led to those artistic masterpieces that have fascinated historians and archaeologists, and attracted millions of tourists.

The rich and evocative symbolism of that now vanished civilisation focused on the immortality of the human spirit, the importance of living a virtuous life, and the reality of judgement for good and bad deeds. The scales of justice appeared in many of the pictograms of Old Egypt that have been preserved and continue to intrigue in modern times.

The spirit is depicted in artwork fluttering like a bird into the joys of the Next World. The Egyptians rightly believed in animal souls, and even had a Cat God that they worshipped every now and again.

NO LOVED ONE IS EVER "LOST"

What becomes of the physical body after death has no bearing on the status or progress of the person who has vacated it and is now safely in the Spirit World, in the company of loved ones. This knowledge should be of great consolation to people who grieve for loved ones whose bodies have never been located.

Their grief is multiplied by the absence of a body to commit to a grave. The denial in such cases of a public day of mourning intensifies the cross that the affected family must bear.

But I can assure all such people that their loved ones have passed safely to a world infinitely more beautiful than the one they have exited so abruptly and unexpectedly.

My clairvoyant vision and trans-sentient perception leaves me in no doubt on this point: Whether a person passes by illness, accident, murder, fire, or drowning, the spirit is indestructible and cannot be harmed by mortal deeds or conduct at the point of physical death.

Even a ferocious bomb explosion that seemingly destroys all trace of a human being will not inflict as much as a scratch on the spirit body. It is immune from earthly damage or annihilation. During my own out of body experiences, I never felt more alive, in my spirit body, despite being detached from its physical counterpart.

You too will feel a sense of liberation and joy after death once you realise that the body that served you during earthly life is no longer necessary-you will know that you are safe and well in the serenity of another world, with a happy get-together involving loved ones to look forward to, followed by a rewarding new life free of pain and earthly restrictions.

Over the years, many people who lost loved ones in shocking, traumatic circumstances have told me of their unbearable grief: The thought of how the person died weighed heavily on their minds.

I assure them that their loved ones are totally healed in the spirit world, regardless of how they passed over, that they are in a different world where the bodies they once occupied on earth have no further relevance to them.

It is only those left behind who fixate on morbid images of coffins and corpses, who mourn the passing of the one who has departed the earth plane. The newly liberated spirit, having completed his or her earthly lifespan, has happily forsaken the Vale of Tears that was life on earth, to begin a far greater, happier, and superior life in the Spirit World.

Never forget that the awful despondency that pervades a funeral parlour, a church during requiem mass, or the melancholy burial scene, is but an illusion: Even as we mourn the passing of a loved one, he or she may be looking on, bemused, at the grief-stricken scenario.

In a way, the wakes that were once an integral part of Irish tradition, but are less common today, had an enlightened approach to death:

Instead of focusing purely on the loss of a loved one, and the sadness of the occasion, people gathered in a room where the earthly body was laid out, and drank whiskey or beer around the corpse. They might sometimes drink a bit too much, but they had the right idea.

They would spend the night reminiscing on the man or woman's good points, or telling stories or yarns about the "dearly departed". Though respecting the dead, they celebrated his or her life in a gentle and good-humoured send off.

That was very much in order, because the great irony of physical death is that it is celebrated on the Other Side – even as we on the earth plane bemoan the passing of a friend or relative.

To loved ones in the Spirit World, the person passing over is greeted as a new arrival, and as someone who has returned from earth after a long absence from "home" – our true home.

Naturally, family members who passed before us are delighted to see us again after a lengthy absence. Why wouldn't they be? And why would they mourn on such a happy occasion?

The opposite applies to the birth of a child. It is a time of rejoicing on earth: A life has begun. The champagne glasses come out, the mother smiles, the family celebrates:

But in the Spirit World tears are shed for the "loss" of a loved one who has departed to begin another life on earth. The departing spirit will not return until after the blessed and liberating moment of death.

The word "dead" itself is misleading in that it implies total destruction. In fact death applies only to the body we cast off. We are very much alive after physical death, animated, conscious of our new surroundings, and full of energy.

But we exist on a different level of being, free from the confines and restrictions of time and space, as we understand these concepts on earth.

We transcend the boundaries and limitations that characterise earthly life, enjoying an infinitely greater freedom in the Spirit World. But we do continue to have bodies – spirit bodies that are perfect.

Our bodies over there will not be subject to illness, disease, injury, deformity, or the all-too familiar aging process. There will be no need to worry about "slowing down", or feeling aches and pains in one's limbs.

There will be no need to reach for the walking stick, or to have one's eyes tested for new spectacles. People who suffer from asthma are among the happiest of all new arrivals on the Other Side-their breathing problems are over! They can bask in the comfort of full health; relieved of the cross they have borne for so long.

The composer Handel's great musical work The Messiah celebrates a futuristic quasi-spiritual scenario in which "the blind can see, the dumb speak, and the ears of the deaf are unstopped".

That vision of release from illness, disease, infirmity, and from the loss of sensory faculties is no mere pipe dream or far flung ecstatic illusion: A blind person who passes over has his eyesight automatically restored ... The deaf person can hear again ... and as for those who were deprived of the power of speech on earth, you just can't shut them up once they leave behind the Vale of Tears and enter ... Paradise.

The greater your suffering and tribulations on this earth, the more you have to look forward to in the life to come.

The question of old age and the loss of what we like to think of as our "good looks" is one that perplexes many people who contemplate the hereafter. If you are one of those who worry about your appearance, or who believes in the importance of "keeping up appearances", you can stop worrying!

Even if we happen to pass over to the Spirit World at an advanced age, we still appear youthful and attractive to those around us, and never grow beyond the age of thirty. We can communicate with others in the Spirit World by normal speech or by telepathy.

And of course we can send messages to those left behind on the earth plane – just as those of you who came to me for readings received messages from loved ones. Though we tend to think of the earth plane and the spirit realms as "worlds apart", they are closer than is often realised. Hence the title of the book!

The Other Side is not located in some far away corner of the universe, beyond the reach of telescopes, or up in the clouds. It is all around us but in another dimension, invisible to the non-clairvoyant, but as solid and as authentic as the physical world we take for granted.

It is so close to us that we don't even need to shout or raise our voices to be heard by our loved ones over there. They are just a whisper away.

When speaking to somebody over the phone, for example, I often receive messages from spirit relatives of the person on the other end of the line. I can tell when a loved one is with the person I am speaking to, and I can hear what that friend or relative in the Spirit World is saying to the telephone caller.

It is the narrow, materialistic view of life and creation that makes it difficult for people to perceive the Greater Reality of other dimensions.

But the truth, the best news of all, awaits you AFTER you draw your last breath!

CHAPTER 7

My Work as a Medium

I F YOU happen to believe in any form of afterlife, then you will probably find it easier to accept that death does not signal the end of a human entity. The real "you" just moves elsewhere, fully intact in a new body and with an expanded consciousness.

You still have all the same likes and dislikes, and more or less the same feelings, emotions, and memories that defined who you were on the earth plane. But, for those left behind, the question arises: Where have you gone if you have survived death? How far away are you in time and space and how is it possible to contact you?

In fact, you are a lot closer to your loved ones when you reach the spirit plane than one might think. You have not been propelled thousands or millions of miles or "light years" away from this planet towards a distant abode above the clouds.

You are not removed or separated from the earth plane in terms of distance … The Spirit World is literally only a whisper away. You visit it dreams when your spirit happily vacates your physical body for a few hours.

You make contact with it simply by thinking of someone you know or care about on the Other Side.

Instead of thinking of a far away place in another galaxy, think of it as existing on another frequency.

As with different wavelengths on a radio set, think of the various higher dimensions as co-existing with our own world rather than located in different parts of the universe. When you are tuned into one radio frequency, you can't listen to another station at the same time, though its transmissions are all around us in the atmosphere.

Any of us, once we cross over, can see and talk to our family or friends on earth. Being on a higher level of existence, we are privileged to be aware of what is happening on the earth plane.

But because few human beings here on earth have developed their psychic potential, it is rare for people still living on the physical plane to have the ability to make the communication a two-way process.

This is where a medium can help: He or she has the power to hear what the spirit people are actually saying, and to pick up messages they wish to pass on to loved ones.

As a medium, I can attune myself to the "frequency" of the Spirit World. I enter a highly receptive state of mind when I go into a light or deep trance.

The latter experience I find draining and exhaustive. The spirit takes me over to such an extent that I relinquish control and let him or her communicate through me. A lighter trance state is adequate in many situations.

On each day that I do readings, I try to avoid heavy meals, confining myself to light sandwiches and fluids. This is necessary, as any clogging in the digestive system can interfere with the process engendered when a spirit temporarily takes over the body of a medium.

Sensations of shock, trauma, fear, and sickness that I experience as the communicating entities relate their earthly causes of death can be quite strong ... the chest expands and other changes occur.

Once a spirit occupies the body, he or she is, for a few seconds or minutes, in partial or complete control, speaking or seeking contact through me.

People at readings tell me they can "see" or "hear" their loved ones when I speak.

What they mean is that they identify the facial expressions, mannerisms, tones and nuances of voice, and accents of the people communicating: A bit like the uncanny similarities that a good mime artist can replicate if she has studied someone and has familiarised herself with every aspect of that person's demeanour, mannerisms, and idiosyncrasies.

Symbols of all the world's great religions adorn the consultation room at Moira's house-cum-clinic.

The difference is that I would not have known by conventional means the spirit person communicating the message. I allow myself to be partially taken over by the spirit to facilitate an evocative and trust-worthier contact with the sitter.

This process is known as "channelling" because it enables departed loved ones to use me as a medium between a sitter and themselves.

To a certain extent, I can re-live the pains and emotions associated with the way they died.

At different times, I have been hanged, shot, drowned, burned, suffocated, or subjected to a taste of what it feels like to pass by the many illnesses that afflict humanity: the cancers, the diseases, the fevers, and the maladies.

I do not get the full brunt of the suffering linked to the "cause of death"-but a strong enough sensory impression of what the person went through to understand how it must have felt to pass by that particular means.

I am taken through the "valley of the shadow of death" and shown exactly what each subject has experienced in passing from the earth plane to the Spirit World. The scenes are re-enacted for me like a televised recording of the ordeals and tribulations undergone by the spirit people who come through.

Possibly the worst sensations that have come to me were those linked to strokes or other sudden impact-related attacks that inflict injury to the head. But we must remember that even with such abrupt or violent forms of departure from the earth plane, it is not death itself that inflicts pain: but the event that causes death.

A spirit feels no pain when it is propelled from the physical body by an accident, sudden death, heart attack, murder, or any other mode of exit from this world. In many cases, the spirit finds itself out of the body even seconds before the moment of impact in a car crash or other such unexpected, violent, or catastrophic occurrence.

Not only is little or no pain involved in sudden death situations. The spirit may find it difficult to believe that death has occurred at all.

Looking down at the crash scene, kitchen floor, hospital bed, or battlefield (in cases of war), he sees the body of someone who, he thinks, looks remarkably like himself. Yet, how can it be? he may ask himself ... when he feels intact ... alive and well.

Once he begins to question his situation, spirit guides or loved ones will be there to offer guidance and direct him to his new life on the Other Side. If the shock of sudden death is overwhelming, the newcomer is cared for in a hospital setting in the Spirit World, and helped every step of the way in adjusting to life "over there".

Getting back to my "spirit table": Sitting opposite me at a reading, you may or may not be aware of the presence of spirit people in the room- depending on your degree of sensitivity.

Many people at readings tell me they experience gentle "swishings" or "touchings" as a session progresses, demonstrating that everyone is psychic to some extent. But I actually see the departed loved ones in the room around the person who has come to me in the hope of hearing about them, or receiving a message from them. Your spirit people will often accompany you when you arrive for a reading.

I pick up the thoughts of the spirit person, who is aware not only of my thoughts but also tuned into the thoughts of the loved one sitting opposite me. This happens after the sitter has shown me a photo of a deceased relative or friend, or asked me to request a communication.

A picture of the spirit person is very helpful. It increases the chances of making contact with the loved one in question.

It is up to the spirit concerned whether to make contact or not. They may choose not to, for reasons of their own. We always have to respect their decision either way.

If somebody comes through, they very often have a strong wish to prove whom they really are. A spirit does this usually by referring to some event, circumstance, or personal curio that only the sitter knows about.

The success of the reading that follows will depend on how competent the medium is, and also to some extent how relaxed and open-minded the sitter happens to be.

If you come for a reading in a very negative state of mind, completely hostile to the idea of life after death and determined not to believe any evidence that might be forthcoming, you may impede the progress of the session.

Even if you are extremely sceptical on these issues – as many people are – it is better to at least be receptive to the POSSIBILITY of spirit communication. That way, you have nothing to lose. You will not be compromising or betraying your beliefs, religious convictions, or indeed an atheistic outlook if that is your disposition.

A good medium is not just one who is deeply receptive to messages from the Spirit World. She must also be an astute interpreter of whatever information is conveyed through her for the sitter. This is where experience and discretion make all the difference.

If the voices are unclear or indistinct, owing perhaps to the energies of the communicating spirit being weak at that particular time, the medium will let you know of the problems arising from this communication problem.

Alternatively, she may attempt to interpret what the message might be, while cautioning you that the resulting analysis is partly conjecture on her part due to difficulty in grasping what the spirit person is attempting to say.

She may base this interpretation on her own judgement, intuition, and enhanced psychic awareness of the Spirit World ... having regard to the overall context of the family situation involved or the nature of the request the sitter has made concerning the departed loved one.

As a natural medium-one born with the ability – I have a clear advantage when it comes to both picking up the spirit messages and interpreting these accordingly.

The psychic skill of each medium varies; just as the level of expertise or efficiency of any one musician or car mechanic differs from others engaged in the same line of work.

But all genuine mediums should be able, in the course of their careers, to demonstrate by their mediumship that there really is a life after death, and also have the capacity to bring comfort and consolation to people who seek reassurance about departed loved ones.

Some mediums specialise in Clairaudience, which even by itself can prove valuable in eliciting information from the spirit world. But the added facility to actually see spirit beings in mental pictures-images in the mind-makes a communication even more special, as it augments the value of the Clairaudient messages.

The ability to attune oneself to the feelings and emotions of a spirit (Clairsentience) further adds to the overall representation of whatever message or thought projection your friend or loved one on the Other Side is attempting to send you.

By combining all my psychic gifts, I find I can render a more complete picture of what comes through at a reading. I pass on whatever thoughts, emotions, audio-messages or symbols I receive from the communicating spirit.

By symbols I mean messages couched in a kind of code that is easy to decipher. For example, if a sitter's loved one in the Spirit World wishes to warn him or her about someone who poses a danger to the family, or who is "just not good enough for them", the communicator may wield a stick, shaking it in condemnatory fashion as a symbol of disapproval and censure.

Whether the concerns are well founded or not, the spirit relative or friend is showing disquiet or apprehension by this gesture. We should bear in mind that when somebody passes over, he or she retains for quite a while the personality traits, attitudes, and behaviour patterns that distinguished him or her on earth.

So if an uncle was bad tempered and moody down here, he might well still be a contrary and disagreeable fellow over there. And if your loved one had deep affection for you on earth, there is no reason to expect that love and care to be any less intense after he/she has made the transition to the Spirit World.

The author's home at Bennettsbridge: Thousands have flocked to this "House of Healing" from all over Ireland and abroad to receive spiritual advice and messages from across the "Great Divide"

Other use of symbolism might involve pictographic images such as bridal gowns, denoting marriage, images associated with various vocations, careers, or professions, or the entrance to a church to symbolise a past or future wedding or funeral or other formal occasion.

Fields of corn, or tractors, could symbolise a spirit's past involvement in farming. If water is shown in connection with a spirit's mode of departure from the earth plane, it could very likely refer to drowning as the cause of death.

If a heart is shown, or I get a mild sensation of pain to the heart, this can refer to heart problems the loved one suffered from, or to a heart attack or failure as the cause of death on the earth plane.

When using the crystal in conjunction with mediumship, symbols also play an important part in the reading. The spirit people can show signs to their loved ones in the crystal.

There is a very good reason why symbolism plays such an important part in spirit communication: The Spirit World, though containing many features that would be familiar to our world, is also vastly different in major respects. Such is the nature of this higher dimension of being that a communicating intelligence must often resort to the use of symbols to convey meanings, to get across a message as clearly as the situation permits.

Where words fail, or seem hopelessly inadequate to express a thought, or to get across a concept of how wonderful life is on the Other Side, mental pictures or symbols may achieve this.

In the same way, the great explorers of the past who discovered new territories often used symbols in an effort to give the natives a rough idea of what the more advanced parts of our world looked like.

Words would have meant nothing, because the unfortunate natives hadn't the slightest notion of what technology was about. So symbolism better served to offer a mental picture of activities that otherwise would have baffled the poor jungle dwellers, mountain tribes, desert nomads or lost tribes out of their wits.

Difficult as verbal or non-verbal exchanges between an advanced earth culture and a primitive or less sophisticated one might seem, it would appear child's play by comparison with trans-dimensional communication: All the more reason to welcome and appreciate the messages that are successfully transmitted to us on the earth plane.

HEALING THE PAIN OF GRIEF

Aside from providing evidence of an afterlife-a crucial aspect of any medium's work, I consider the HEALING potential of each reading to be of paramount importance.

One cannot ever underestimate or understate the enormous, mind-blowing, life-changing significance of contact established with the Spirit World ... of hearing once again from a person you may have seen laid out in a funeral parlour ... and buried in a graveyard amidst tears of sadness and grieving.

You know then that it was a mortal body you saw, not the person you knew and cared about. He or she has simply moved on.

Though you may read these words, and thumb through the chapters of this book, whether believing, disbelieving, or totally rejecting the concept of life after death, you have to experience FIRST HAND a reading in which a spirit person makes contact IN ORDER TO UNDERSTAND AND TAKE ON BOARD THE FACT THAT THERE IS A WORLD ELSEWHERE IN WHICH ALL YOUR LOVED ONES CONTINUE TO EXIST, AND TO LIVE THEIR LIVES.

It is when a loved one on the Other Side contacts the person sitting opposite me for the reading that healing begins! Tears flow. Moved, and incredulous, the man or woman may reach for the box of tissues.

There may be sobbing ... a healthy symptom of emotional release. All those pent-up emotions, unresolved grievances, regrets, and half forgotten memories of the loved one come flooding back. I have witnessed and experienced the healing potential of trans-dimensional contact on countless occasions: In one reading, a woman whose children died in a house fire came to me, hoping to receive a message ... or a sign of some kind ... from the loved ones who had been so tragically snatched from her.

She was ecstatic when her children came through. She knew they were safe in the Spirit World despite the horrific manner of their passing.

She felt overwhelming relief. But what really delighted the mother was to learn that her children had met a very special person on the Other Side.

They revealed that Princess Dianna had consoled and comforted them. The lady found this news exhilarating. Dianna, in her earthly life, had been a great friend to children the world over, and had worked tirelessly for child protection causes worldwide.

From that day onwards, she would know and understand that her little ones were not lost forever ... but happily awaiting her own eventual crossing to the Spirit World where the family would be re-united.

Entering Bennettsbridge, Co. Kilkenny, the village Moira has taken to her heart.

Even people who like to maintain a "brave face" and a stiff upper lip, never displaying a sign of emotion in their daily lives, can break down in tears when that departed old friend or relative sends a greeting to them across the Great Divide.

It is a fact that many people attend a funeral of a loved one without shedding a tear. They hold back their true feelings for weeks, months, or even years. Hearing from the person in the Spirit World helps to break down a barrier and release the bottled-up or unexpressed emotions that need to be expressed and acted out for healing to commence.

That is what truly makes my work as a medium worthwhile: This healing of hurt minds, grief-stricken human beings, and bereaved families. It brings to them the ultimate and most comforting form of closure: the knowledge that their loved ones are not "gone forever", but alive and well in a better world.

CHAPTER 8

My Spirit Guide

MY SPIRIT guide is a Red Indian. He has been helping and guiding me for many years. Three feathers protrude from his beautiful headdress of multi-coloured plumage that reaches to his heels. He has given me support and strength during all my readings and also protects me from dark forces.

In native American art and culture, spirit guides were represented by animal forms and totemic symbols.

He has on some occasions placed a golden cloak around me for protection. Such a protective shield is very necessary during spiritual readings to prevent any malevolent or un-evolved entities from interfering in the channelling process.

Many mediums down through history have emphasised the value and importance of having a guide from the Other Side to help keep them focused on the task of facilitating contact. The guide is referred to in psychic literature as a doorkeeper who guards and protects a medium during trance.

In the case of non-psychics, the guide looks after one's spiritual interests up to a certain point ... stopping short of intervening in a way that would compromise or dilute our entitlement to free will on the earth plane.

Some mediums refer to their guides as people in the Spirit World who act as "Masters of Ceremonies", in the sense that they introduce spirit beings and "screen" the various spirit people anxious to communicate with somebody on earth.

The guide can ensure that the medium avoids the hazards and pitfalls that any person in trance may face if unprepared for the challenging process of spirit communication. Apart from my guide, I can see many other helpful spirit people and angels around me.

We all have spirit guides ... though in most cases people are unaware of these constant companions and advisers. They help us by "pointing the way" for us throughout life, but don't compel us to follow any particular course of action. Free will reigns supreme.

Because people are so busy nowadays, rushing around and coping with the pressures of a hi-tech society, they many not be as sensitive or open to the communications from their guides.

But the guides still "get through". Very often, what you think of as an instinct or an intuitive or discerning thought may actually be a helpful tip or wise counsel from your guide.

In dreams especially they communicate with the greatest of ease. In this twilight zone between sleeping and waking, people are more attuned to the higher realms than when we are going about our daily work or recreational routines.

Messages can come in pictures, words, or symbols, depending on the individual who is receiving the advice or information.

Some people think more in words than in pictures, so whatever mode of communication is best suited to a person is the one that will be applied. The help provided by spirit guides is valuable, indeed essential, to every human being, but is mostly taken for granted:

Spirits abound in Moira's presence. Here, some of them achieve partial visibility at her home in Bennettbridge, Co. Kilkenny.

Spirit forms appear in a photo of Moira's mother, Katie Purcell-Geoghegan.

Spirit energies: Note the light forms on either side of the doorway.

A spirit presence manifests in a photo of Moira's daughter, Sharon.

They watch over us, help us to avert danger ... maybe steer us towards people we need to meet, or away from those we should be avoiding-though again, we have to make the ultimate decisions ourselves no matter how rational or level-headed their "nudges" or inspiration may be.

They will never pressurise or manipulate you into opting for X or Y when it comes to making a crunch decision. I can consciously consult and listen to my Spirit Guide, which is of course a rare gift.

Being Clairvoyant and Clairaudient, I can see and hear my Red Indian guide from the Spirit World. But anyone reading this book has the potential to develop a greater awareness of his or her guide.

The author's grandson, Joseph: Moira perceives the faces of family members on the illuminated part of the door to the right.

By meditating, you can open your hearts and minds to these wonderful life-long invisible friends who care so deeply about you.

Your spirit guide can be someone you knew in a previous life, or in the Spirit World before incarnating for your present round of challenges. He or she may be a person who was a family member during a previous incarnation. Whoever it is, your guide is always there to help ... discreetly and unseen, but with eternal wisdom and compassion.

CHAPTER 9

Children who Pass Over

P ERHAPS the greatest, most painful blow a parent can suffer is the loss of a child, whether as a baby or after the son or daughter has been in the family for a number of years.

A question I am asked often is what happens to these loved ones ... children who appear to have been snatched cruelly and without any reason or justification from a loving home.

The honest answer, based on my direct perception and experience of the Spirit World, is that loving and highly trained people welcome these children once they cross over, including in many cases family members already on the Other Side.

They are cared for in nurseries and allowed to grow in the Spirit World to the age of about 21- to full adulthood. They then get various jobs to do, such as looking after people on the Earth Plane.

The spirit children of mothers who have miscarried or caused "terminations" do not judge them in the way that some people on earth do. They understand, and forgive ... if forgiveness is necessary or required. Angel children who were deprived of the power of speech in their earthly lives have this faculty restored to them in spirit. Likewise with other illnesses that may have afflicted or held them back them on earth: when they enter the Spirit World, they leave behind all pain and earthly suffering and are healed of whatever illness they and their families had to cope with.

I have been allowed to see people in the Spirit World who are about to be born. I have seen children with different or special needs and I can honestly say that families who receive such children are gifted and privileged.

God has chosen them to receive special children. In some cases, the children may have only a short time to live, but I believe the host families are picked by God to care for them.

Families who care for special needs children deserve our respect, admiration, and where appropriate, our support. They are meeting a great and noble challenge with honour and dignity, and great will be their reward in the afterlife.

MOTHERS FORCED TO GIVE UP BABIES IN YOUTH

I've met mothers in their fifties or sixties who were forced to give up babies in the days when having children out of wedlock attracted social stigma and was deemed a terrible sin.

Many such women developed psychiatric problems in later life or suffered from deep depression.

They long to see their children again. A heartless society inflicted an unfair and unmerited burden on these innocent women. My message to those loving, caring women is simple and straightforward:

YOU are not to blame for the wrong that was done to you.

Your children are not lost: they are angels.

76

Don't be put off, or bothered in the slightest, by the misguided notions of "sin" promulgated by holier than thou churchmen, and their allies, the professional gossipers and self-righteous accusers who liked to boost their own egos by downing anyone who didn't measure up to their unnatural expectations.

You are the ones who know the truth. You are deserving of recognition and due admiration for the love you bestowed on the child you brought into this world.

The back-stabbers and malicious scandal mongers who seek to denigrate your sacrifice and your compassionate natures will have to answer one day for their selfishness ... for their hurtful, vindictive attempts to misrepresent your courage and dignity.

Your children will forgive you if you reach out to them. If they have passed to the Spirit World, you can still send thoughts and messages of love to them.

ABORTION AND THE SPIRIT WORLD

Abortion has been the subject of a raging controversy in Ireland and elsewhere in recent years. Opinions are sharply divided on the issue.

Some people feel a woman should be judged harshly for seeking a termination. Others see it as a difficult, painful, justifiable if regrettable way of dealing with an unwanted pregnancy.

I have had women for readings who went through the termination ordeal. They spoke of the lengthy and agonising decision-making process that preceded their trips to England, the fears and lingering tortuous doubts during the sea crossing ... and the heartbreaking visit to the clinic where the operations were performed.

I believe anyone who finds herself in this situation deserves compassion, support, and understanding-and not a judgemental attitude – from other members of society not confronted by the dilemmas that face women with unwanted pregnancies.

An angel carries a child to the peace and glory of the Spirit World.

The woman who undergoes the termination ordeal has to live with her choice, and it may cause her a lot of trauma, sadness, regret, depression, or misplaced guilt in the months and years following the ordeal.

Seen from a spiritual vantage point, however, the whole termination experience takes on a different gist and implication.

As a medium, I can assure readers that each and every unborn child affected by a termination returns to the Spirit World where he or she grows to maturity. I have seen some of these children.

Though their entry into our world has been cut short, this process does not harm them. They are quickly restored to a safe and healing environment on the Other Side where they are cared for by relatives or other spirit people.

One woman who had undergone five secret abortions came to me for a reading. She had told nobody in her family about these.

Her grandmother came through and informed her that she was looking after five children in the Spirit World. These, she added, were the woman's grandchildren who were happily growing up since being "terminated" on the earth plane.

Hearing this news from her grandmother, the woman became emotional and almost fell asunder with the shock. Regaining her composure, she wiped away the tears and explained that she never expected her secret to be revealed, and certainly not by her deceased grandmother speaking from the Spirit World!

It should be remembered that a termination, like any other traumatic incident or experience in life; can help a woman to grow in wisdom and understanding. It may have been sent as a cross to bear or an obstacle to overcome as part of the learning process that is central to all incarnations on the earth plane.

CHAPTER 10

Suicide

MUCH HAS been written and broadcast about the issue of suicide. Medical and psychiatric reports have been published worldwide, and there are very good information leaflets available from health boards that offer both advice to relatives of suicide victims, and help to people who may be contemplating suicide.

As a medium with direct personal knowledge of what follows physical death, I have my own perspective on the subject. I have been permitted to see, and hear from, people of all ages who have passed by suicide. From what has been shown to me, I have some simple and direct advice for anyone thinking of "ending it all": Don't do it!

In the past, and still to a certain extent today, families go into denial about suicides and try to conceal the tragedies from neighbours and the wider community. Even within the family circle, it may not be spoken about.

The true cause of death is so difficult to confront and come to terms with that it may not be alluded to in obituaries, funeral masses, or in everyday conversation.

In some cases, whole generations of a family are brought up to believe that a relative who passed by suicide died from an illness or disease.

Sadly, a sense of shame and guilt motivated this silence that shrouded the sudden and unexpected departure of a loved from the earthly plane. Very often, families feared that the suicide might reflect badly on the victim's home or upbringing.

Attitudes to suicide were not helped by the practise within the Catholic Church of refusing to allow victims to be interred on consecrated ground. This policy added to the grief and suffering of relatives, who had this unjust and painful stigma to cope with on top of the sudden death of a loved one.

Though it was perfectly justified in discouraging suicide, the Church displayed a frightening lack of sensitivity in its implementation of heartless, man-made laws that had nothing to do with an all-loving and compassionate God.

It overlooked the traumatic effects of its teachings on the families of suicide victims.

Thankfully, the Church has now relaxed its harsh policy on suicides, and we seldom hear nowadays of anyone being denied a decent Christian burial. This change of heart on the part of the Church Hierarchy at least helps to remove part of the stigma that attached to suicide in the past.

In Ireland, it is believed that the incidence of suicide is under-reported, but we know from the confirmed cases that it has become the principal cause of death among young people.

Though it is important never to make suicide look like an acceptable or ethical way out of an earthly challenge, we should always show compassion and understanding to the family of the victim, and avoid creating any sense of stigma around the person who has opted to end his life.

A person may resort to suicide for a variety of reasons: alcohol abuse, job loss, anger, guilt, a humiliating experience, depression, a loss of hope, bereavement, loneliness, to name a few of the most commonly cited causes or contributory factors.

If you are considering suicide, I urge you to reflect on the consequences, firstly for yourself, and secondly for your loved ones who will be devastated and traumatised. If you take this drastic and irreversible step, you will be opting out of a life and a set of challenges that you choose for yourself before you entered the earthly plane.

Suicide has rightly been defined as "a permanent solution to a temporary problem." And so it is, because when the victim arrives on the Other Side, he sees just how unwise and pointless his action has been.

Most of the problems that drive people to suicide can be resolved simply by seeking help and advice.

It is the feeling that nobody cares, or that there is no one to turn to; that needs to be overcome. Whatever the stimulus that leads to premature ending of an earth life, it seems very small indeed when you arrive in the Spirit World and realise the gravity of the act.

Then it becomes clear that there was no need or justification for such a drastic exit from the earth plane.

There is a feeling of overwhelming remorse once you realise the full impact of the decision to end your life: Apart from cutting short your allotted earthly life span-a bit like quitting school before the end of term, you have to take responsibility for the grief, distress, and unbearable sorrow you have visited on family and friends.

Without exception, suicide victims say they regret their actions and insist that they would not resort to the same act if they could live their lives over again. They seek forgiveness.

They say they didn't realise the horrendous, far-reaching consequences of their decision at the time.

But after healing and counselling, they see their act in a different light and send apologies to their families on earth. They express deep and sincere regret for the grief and devastation their sudden departure from the earth plane has caused.

A PERSONAL DECISION – NOBODY ELSE TO BLAME

Without exception also, they tell me that it was THEIR OWN DECISION, and theirs alone, to take their lives, and that no one else ought to be blamed. They wish to accept responsibility so that no one left behind has to suffer feelings of guilt and self-recrimination.

It is a known fact that most people, at some point in their lives, contemplate suicide. There are so many pressures and challenges to contend with that the option of suicide seems tempting in certain situations.

Some suicides might have been avoided if there had been proper guidance or help to tide them over the crisis, depression, or bad patch that afflicted them.

Unfortunately, even the closest friends or family members may not have been aware of the inner turmoil being experienced by the person thinking of suicide. He or she may appear outwardly normal in all respects, so that the suicide comes as a complete shock to everybody.

So, please, do not attempt to judge somebody who commits suicide. He or she will come to terms with the act and receive healing in the Spirit World. Help and support friends or family members affect by suicide.

Coma and Alzheimer's

CHAPTER 11

Coma and Alzheimer's

THERE ARE many myths and misunderstandings concerning such dreaded conditions as Coma and Alzheimer's. From a conventional medical viewpoint, there is much that remains unexplained about the nature of these mysterious afflictions. A lot of research will be needed to get to the heart of what exactly they are and how to cure the unfortunate victims.

The effect on relatives of those afflicted is far-reaching and devastating. A patient who has entered a comatose state appears to just lie there, without apparent movement ... lifeless ... apart from the tubes and advanced medical paraphernalia that keep him "ticking over" in the hope that he may one day emerge from the coma.

Every visit to the hospital is an ordeal that can become a drab and seemingly pointless routine. Loved ones stand by the bedside and speak to the inert, immobile human form with all those gadgets protruding from what, in the estimation of many people, might as well be a corpse. They speak words of comfort and consolation, perhaps talk about old times and the good old days before the accident or illness intervened to shatter a life and break the hearts of all who knew the victim. They speak, wishing to God their words could be heard by that friend or relative who has passed into a deep sleep from which he or she may never awaken.

Sometimes, they dare to hope that maybe ... just maybe ... their words spoken with love and quiet desperation have not been in vain, but have somehow penetrated the veil that separates the mundane world from the realms of that feared, silent, seemingly unreachable state of being we refer to as COMA.

Often, when exiting the hospital after yet another visit, a family member is prompted to ask, out loud or in a whisper: "I could have sworn he smiled, or that he heard me that time".

I have been asked a thousand times about this. As a psychic and a medium, can I answer the sixty four thousand Euro question: "Can they hear us?"

The good news is that they can!

At many readings, spirit people who died after finally slipping away from a comatose state that may have lasted weeks, months or years come through to assure their loved ones that THEY KNEW EVERYTHING THAT WAS GOING ON, AND THAT NOT A WORD OF WHAT WAS SAID IN THEIR PRESENCE PASSED THEM BY!

It must be remembered that a person in a coma, like a person who is asleep or unconscious, is still a human being; in other words, a SPIRIT with a body like the rest of us. Though his or her physical body may be out of action, the spirit, which is the REAL you or me, has not been harmed or incapacitated in the slightest degree.

As in the cases of near death experiences, the spirit of a comatose patient is fully alert and conscious of his/her surroundings. If anything, you may achieve a heightened state of awareness in that situation because you have temporally vacated the dense weighty frame that serves as a vehicle for your spirit during life on earth.

So always know that your dear friend or family member reclining in that hospital bed is not just a lifeless lump of protoplasm.

He or she is a human being with human feelings and concerns, who is, for whatever reason, undergoing the challenge of being placed in, or assigned to, that testing circumstance.

An important point about coma: It does not mean necessarily that the patient is being punished for any offence committed in this or a previous life. It may well be the loved ones who are being tested by the situation.

In life, we all learn through adversity and failure, as well as through love and achievement. As I state elsewhere in this book, we are all born with a map. Every experience, good and bad, painful or pleasurable, negative or life enhancing, has a purpose.

It is only at the end of life's long drawn-out meandering adventure that we see the whole picture. Then, all the pieces of the jigsaw fit together. We achieve a perfect understanding of what it was all about.

Every challenge thrown up along life's obstacle course provides us with opportunities for growth and spiritual advancement. The coma has to be seen in that light.

And of course a comatose person who passes over while in the condition is fully healed in the Spirit World, where every tear is wiped away and all illness banished to oblivion.

Be careful too about assuming that people who suffer from Alzheimer's cannot hear or understand what is going on around them. They understand a great deal more than onlookers appreciate, even if they cannot express themselves in a way that the average person identifies with.

Some time ago, I had a woman for a reading who wondered if she might hear from her deceased mother who had been an Alzheimer's patient in her declining years. Given the perceived nature of this illness, the woman wanted go be assured that her mother was now at peace and healed on the other side.

A surprise lay in store for this client: Not only was the dearly departed lady in full possession of her senses, and more alert than ever:

The spirit revealed that she had, in her final years on earth, been aware all along of the behaviour of other people around her, including her daughter (who was sitting there in front of me), and often heard exactly what they were saying about her!

But a bigger shock was to come. She told her daughter, through me, that she was unhappy with her for giving away jewellery and other possessions of hers, instead of distributing these to members of the family.

The woman was full of remorse when she heard this, apologised to her mother, and promised to respect her feelings. A year or so later, the lady phoned me to confirm that she had rectified matters in accordance with her mother's wishes regarding the property and possessions.

This situation ought to serve as a cautionary tale for anyone who believes that Alzheimer's sufferers can be taken for granted or treated as if they were "completely out of it". We should respect their presence and basic human dignity and not behave as though they didn't exist.

There is a perception, based on ignorance and misunderstanding; that they are in a Zombie like state that admits of no direct awareness of the world around them.

This is far from the case. They are human beings like ourselves – but have taken on this particular cross to bear. They are learning from their experience of the illness, as surely as the family members or carers learn from looking after them.

Though afflicted by a condition that prevents them from being cognisant of reality in a way that the rest of us can fathom or appreciate, they are conscious of their environment in other, more profound ways.

Their physical brains may be affected by the ailment, but their immortal spirits are untainted and undaunted by this purely temporary block to their ability to give utterance to their innermost thoughts and participate in the general run of worldly existence.

Once free of their mortal bodies, and safely back in the Spirit World, they are one hundred percent cured and once again able to converse, not only with their loved ones "over there", but also, as the above reading demonstrates, with relatives back on Earth.

CHAPTER 12

The Spirit World: Beautiful beyond your wildest dreams!

O NE PARTICULARLY striking feature of the Spirit World is the far greater range and variety of colours that shimmer and sparkle and illuminate every part of it. And the intensity of the hues, tones, and shades would dazzle the eyes of anyone still on the physical plane.

The sky has rich colour nuances and gradations of a kind unknown to the sensory faculties most people use on this planet. As well as brilliant shades of blue and calming light reds, it exudes a multitude of other colours that add to the overall sense of well-being and contentment on the Other Side.

A sun does not provide light in the Spirit World, as on this plane. But what some mystics refer to as the "astral light" never fades and offers perfect illumination that is never too dim or too bright.

The scenery and countryside environment of the Spirit World is beautiful beyond description. A set of postcards I picked up a few years ago depicting dream landscapes came close-or as close as an artist possibly can get- to offering a glimpse of what the afterlife terrain looks like:

The cards show an idyllic countryside, dotted with forests, hedgerows, lakes, happily grazing animals, with spirit people enjoying the peace and freedom from strife that characterise the higher levels of existence: Nature in its purest form or manifestation, without any of its negative aspects.

The flowers and other forms of plant life are larger, more attractive, and shimmer with all the bright, scintillating colours of the rainbow. This is how the Spirit World looks: It resembles an enhanced, improved, vastly upgraded version of our own world.

I remember one meditation I underwent during which I found myself transported to a beautiful spot on the Other Side.

I passed between two opalescent pillars that towered far above my height. They reminded me of the columns that supported the Roman Coliseum, or those lofty temples of ancient Greece that elicited the wonder and admiration of the Western World.

Having come through this numinous opening or gateway, I sat down beside a pond that seemed to live and breathe with abundance of sub aquatic vegetation that the clear still water made visible. The pool was encircled by vibrantly toned foliage and shrubbery. A feeling of total serenity came over me.

A scene to gladden the heart: The River Nore at Bennettsbridge, Co. Kilkenny. The Spirit World looks even better than this!

As I rested by the side of this pond, I wondered what on earth I was doing here. Then, a spirit person approached and handed me a Water Lilly. It was gigantic, many times the size of its earthly counterpart.

As I took it from him, he explained that my passing through the pillars was symbolic of a "breakthrough" I had made in my own life. I had pierced another of those barriers that confront us all in the course of our earthly journey.

This experience is typical of the composed, visually stunning, and memorable scenes that greet a visitor to one of the higher levels of being.

People who have enjoyed even one such glimpse of the "Other World" say it has changed their lives, and that they will never forget what they saw until their dying day.

Yet no words adequately describe how glorious and breathtakingly superb it actually is. You'll find that out when you get there.

It is the multi-coloured vibrancy and splendour of that Far Country, our true HOME that inspires my own love of colour. People often remark on the colour scheme of my house in Bennettsbridge: It has been a talking point among passers-by for years. It never fails to catch the eye, even if opinions differ as to its aesthetic or polychromatic appeal!

That's a matter of taste, of course, but for me it represents an imitation, however pallid or inadequate, of what I see in the Spirit World when I survey its delightful terrain.

HOUSES IN THE SPIRIT WORLD?

Speaking of houses, people wonder if we can live in a house in the Spirit World. The good news is that there are houses and homes in the Other Side as on earth. The disturbing notion that one just wanders aimlessly after death in a strange misty land "somewhere up there", playing a harp most of the time or vaguely thinking about eternity, is just a myth.

People have reflected sadly and bitterly on the idea that they would never again see, or live in, the type of house they loved while on earth, or exist in the kind of soothing or agreeable urban or rural environmental setting to which they have become accustomed throughout decades of life on earth.

Centuries of conditioning and well meaning but misguided sermonising have helped to foster such bleak expectations and misconceptions.

It comes as a pleasant and welcome surprise to people crossing over when they find the Spirit World dotted with beautiful houses. These may be grouped together in little villages or communes, or you can have a house positioned in a setting that might strike others as unusual but that you personally find pleasing and appropriate.

It is equally true that we do not need to live in houses if we dislike the idea. The afterlife realms abound with buildings of all sorts, ranging from humble cabins or cottages to sprawling mansions and palaces.

These can be constructed from what appear to be actual building materials but spirit communicators also speak of creating our dwelling places in the afterlife by thought alone.

They have described through mediums an astonishing process by which highly evolved spirit people create breathtakingly beautiful buildings by vibrational thought-waves and energies.

The design and overall appearance of a person's home in the Spirit World often reflects his or her level of spiritual advancement. You can live in a dwelling designed by yourself or one conceived and built (or thought-constructed) by someone else-perhaps someone with superior architectural skills.

You can have the garden of your choice-if you like gardens. This, and the furnishings in your home, will be determined by your state of mind and your inner needs or preferences.

It is common for a person's departed loved ones to create an exact replica of his or her home on earth as a surprise for them when they arrive.

After a while, some spirits give up the earthly attachment to living in a house and opt to be as "free as the wind", moving to whatever location or setting takes their fancy. In the Spirit World, there is no need to shelter from the elements-you won't get caught in a shower or hailstorm on the Other Side- and there is no fear or threat of criminal activity.

So houses are really a luxury. Some people might be found surrounded by flowers and animals, but not bothering with a house. Their place of residence could consist of a beautiful garden patch, the side of a mountain, a picturesque spot in some dreamlike setting, or indeed any location or environment of their choosing.

But the homes of spirit people are nonetheless very real. They are as solid and authentic to them as our own homes are to us on earth ... just more comfortable and more attractive.

There are no pest control problems ... no bugs or rodents trouble us and there is no need to reach for a sweeping brush or vacuum cleaner, or to wash the floors or dust the shelves.

We can relax, or entertain friends or family in our homes on the Other Side. Locks and bolts are unnecessary, as burglars are non-existent. There is no need for safes and moneyboxes either as money has value only on the earth plane.

CLOTHING?

There are no restrictions on the style or variety of clothing in the Spirit World. As with your immediate environment and the house you choose to live in, you can decide exactly what clothes you wish to wear. You will find every conceivable form of clothing on the other side. Generally, it seems that the closer you are to the earth plane, the greater the similarity of one's spirit apparel.

You can wear what you consider your "own clothes" for as long as you wish – or for as long as you feel comfortable with them. But after a while you may feel the urge to dispense with your earth garments and replace these with outfits or costumes more in keeping with your changing circumstances and perspectives.

It is a common sight to see people constantly changing what they wear as they experience changes in thinking or move to higher levels of existence in the afterlife.

Other spirits create the actual clothing for newcomers, or, in the case of people with strong and vivid imaginations, the new arrivals themselves can conjure up the suits, dresses, and whatever they desire.

Clothing is not made out of fabrics or materials, but fashioned from one's own inner desires and emotions. It never gets dirty and doesn't ever require washing or repairing.

Instead of working for hours to produce the garments, the spirit people simply gather the necessary elements from the surrounding atmosphere and weave these into the visible fabrics that adorn the occupants of their world.

Clothing is often prepared in advance in the spirit world for people who are due to cross over. They know of our impending departure from the earth plane for quite a while before death and ensure that such considerations will be well looked after.

To a certain extent, our spiritual clothing will correspond to our level of advancement and evolution-our spiritual progress. It may change as we change our attitudes and move forward in terms of moral and emotional development.

Our particular status, and the work we are assigned to do, as well as our emotional state, will be reflected in the colour, style, fashion and textures of the clothing we choose.

You can dress in formal wear or opt for loose fitting, ceremonial dress such as flowing robes that denote grace and refinement.

As one ascends through the various levels of the Spirit World, one's clothing appears lighter and more vivid.

People who achieved a high degree of saintliness on earth tend to be seen wearing a form of clothing that reflects their inner purity, wisdom, and compassion. Their bodies radiate heavenly qualities and rays of light may appear to reflect from them.

Immensely wise men and women often opt for robes of sapphire blue and their brilliant auras, like those of the saints depicted in old paintings, shine through. The choice of clothing may vary, depending on the trends, fashions and preferences that dominated the span of one's earth life.

But certain forms of clothing have a timeless appeal due to their historic association with a particular state of mind or disposition. A medium in 1927, for example, described women in the Spirit World who had beautiful long hair flowing over their shoulders and wore soft rose coloured sandals.

He saw young girls that seemed to be shrouded in white dresses with flowers, denoting innocence. The men, he noticed, wore casual clothing or formal dress, as they wished, and many of them sported hats ... less common nowadays.

It must be remembered that clothing on the Other Side is fashioned, not from man-made fabrics, but from the wonderful atmospheric thought energies of the Spirit World.

DO WE EAT AND DRINK?

As with clothing, food in the Spirit World is created by thought energies.

It can be enjoyed without the hassle and irritation of cooking and is not produced in kitchens or by long and arduous methods of preparation that require chefs and cooks, sowing of fruit and vegetables, or the farming and slaughter of livestock.

No matter how like earth food it may seem, this rule applies: The meat you chose to enjoy has not necessitated the killing of any living creature, and there is no possibility of eating anything poisonous, because the food does not contain any of the impurities common to the earth plane.

Of course, if you have enjoyed cooking while on earth-as distinct from seeing it as a chore- you can prepare food in that way in the Spirit World

You don't actually need to eat on the other side. It is purely for pleasure or comfort that you partake of food. Eating is more of a priority for us when we first arrive on the Other Side.

But as we grow accustomed to our spirit life, we may decide to dispense with the habit. One can instead just absorb nutrients from the atmosphere, without the requirement to chew or digest anything.

Seasoned drinkers could be disappointed, however, as all reports suggest that alcohol is not permitted in the Spirit World, though all forms of non-intoxicating fluids are available.

As a mind-changing drug, its effects would be totally at odds with the feeling of well-being and serenity that prevails over there. Likewise, there is no dope such as Heroin or marijuana to wreak the kind of damage and heartbreak these substances cause on the earth plane.

Some diehard or severely addicted drinkers get around the absence of drink by returning to earth from time to time and entering pubs they used to frequent before passing over.

Unseen by the "regulars" in the pub, they can imbibe the fumes of the alcohol and get quite a buzz from it, similar to the intoxicating effects of normal drinking.

On anniversaries, spirit people may re-visit old haunts and knock back a few "drinks" before returning to the Spirit World. I do not recommend this practise.

WORK AND CREATIVITY "OVER THERE"

If you worry that there will be nothing for you to do in the Spirit World but sing hymns and pray all the time, you're in for a pleasant surprise.

There are many tasks to which you can apply yourself, a dazzling range of activities to occupy your "time" in a world where time itself, as we know it down here, has no meaning. You can be involved in research work aimed at helping inhabitants of the physical plane.

Mediums worldwide have relayed graphic descriptions of marble buildings, gorgeous palaces and towers, libraries, cathedrals of light, and awe-inspiring centres of learning.

Within the walls of these magnificent abodes countless thousands of evolved spirits attend to their studies, literary pursuits, or creative endeavours.

Others devote themselves to grandiose projects that would beggar the imaginations or intellectual capacities of our planet's most brilliant minds.

Reference has also been made in spirit communication to unearthly structures that radiate undreamt of architectural beauty and perfection.

Interestingly, in struggling to find words to describe the appearance of certain buildings in a way that people on earth can understand or identify with, spirit communicators have, over the decades, referred to a "mother of pearl" like façade or exterior, or to a "pearly" appearance.

This should give us food for thought: Perhaps this is where the popular term "Pearly Gates" originated ... in the Spirit World itself! People joke every day of the week about Saint Peter and the Pearly Gates, without reflecting that one fine day, at some point in the future, they will have a chance to check them out ... personally.

Vast numbers of spirit people are engaged in furthering the scientific, intellectual and philosophical progress of humankind. Some of them concentrate on sending guidance and inspiration to people on earth who are engaged in similar spheres of activity.

You will have heard or read of somebody who was wracking his brains down here, doggedly seeking the solution to a complex problem or situation ... only to have it solved miraculously in a dream or in a flash of intuition or insight.

That is very often the result of helpful intercession by spirit beings, directing their knowledge and superior wisdom towards the mind of the perplexed human with a view to enhancing his or her understanding of an issue ... or even to achieve total success in whatever venture, project, or research the person is engaged in.

Throughout history, there have been instances of people notching up successes in all spheres of human activity due to such spirit guidance.

In the Spirit World, great minds are always at work inspiring people in positions of influence. Unfortunately, much of the helpful tips and potentially powerful guidance is ignored, or is not taken on board by the recipient earthly minds.

If you were artistically inclined on earth, you can continue to pursue that interest. Painters, and colour buffs will love the limitless possibilities that open up for them in the Spirit World.

The vastly expanded colour spectrum includes tints, hues, shades, and combinations unknown to the physical plane because these are on a higher vibratory level. Imaginations can run riot when it comes to painting great works of art in a world where the mind, and the power of thought, reign supreme.

Artists in the Spirit World who are no longer restricted by the five sensory faculties that, on earth, might have limited the scope of their vision and creative genius ... create staggeringly beautiful masterpieces.

Some of the truly magnificent art works on earth down through the centuries are believed by psychics to have been influenced by artistic minds in the Spirit World.

Of course, it would have been impossible for the original work, as executed in the higher dimension of spirit to be reproduced down here ... but even a pale imitation of what has been created on the Other Side will draw gasps of admiration on the earth plane.

And the sound of music in Paradise is truly "out of this world". In scripture and the reported visions of psychics, you may have read about the Choirs of Angels who sing "Hosannas" in praise of the Creator. Those evocative descriptions were not fantastical or fictional ravings-but vivid and true accounts of another world.

You can look forward to hearing the sweet music of the cosmic symphonies ... or any kind of musical sounds or expressions that resonate in harmony with your own personal preferences or needs.

Immense concert halls echo to the most ineffably awe-inspiring and evocative works, composed in many cases by spirit people who were once famed and feted on earth for their creative masterpieces.

Poets are well and truly "in Heaven" in the Spirit World.

Here, they can find the means to express all those thoughts, ideas, and emotions in words ... they can articulate or give artistic expression in ways unknown upon the earth plane.

Words that might have seemed hollow, inapt, or devoid of the precise meaning the poet had in mind resonate with meaning in the spiritual realms.

Poetry-and indeed story telling and all forms of literary activity- lives and breathes and inspires ... not just in the great centres of learning and recreation, but in the hearts, minds and dwelling places of spirit people who love or appreciate the craft of the writer and his/her ability to sculpt with words and language.

PEOPLE YOU DISLIKE –
YOU CAN'T MEET THEM "OVER THERE"!

You can avoid people you dislike or don't feel comfortable with in the Spirit World. The Law of Harmony prevents you from encountering anyone that distresses you or with whom you are in disharmony. Personality clashes are alien to the Spirit World. The principle of "like attracts like" prevails ... to everyone's advantage.

Actually, one of the reasons we are born on the earth plane is that certain lessons we need to learn necessitate coming into contact with people we don't like.

Since we cannot experience on the Other Side the kind of conflict generated by discord, fights, marriage break-up, family feuds, petty hatreds, and all the other tension-fraught situations common to the earth plane, we have to come down here to get a hefty dose of the sensations and emotions, and opportunities for spiritual growth, that such unpleasant but maturing ordeals provide us with.

On earth, we have to learn through suffering and hardship ... as well as through love and kindness. But while we can experience plenty of the latter in the Spirit World, we have to come to the School of Life down here to get all the hard knocks and have our rough edges smoothed off.

Thus we grow and evolve, through many lives, until we have advanced to a point where further earth incarnations are unnecessary. How long it takes us to reach that point of liberation from the cycle of birth, death, and rebirth is up to ourselves.

In the meantime, we can look forward to our "end of term breaks" in the Spirit World, while striving to be better, more caring people on earth.

CHAPTER 13

Born with a Map

THE COSMIC pattern formed by the position of the planets at birth contributes to the formation of your personality. A reasonably clear picture emerges for the trained astrologer of your character, general disposition, emotional traits, special gifts, and other facets of your physical and psychological composition.

If supplied with precise and reliable information on the planetary positions at your time of birth, an astrologer can draft a horoscope setting out in considerable detail the probable course of your life.

The horoscope indicates possible pitfalls to be avoided, and likely defeats and triumphs, likes and dislikes, strengths and weaknesses associated with your particular astrological make-up.

It may be difficult for the average person to make any sense of this notion: that the movements and alignments of far-away planets can influence human behaviour.

But consider the proven effects of the moon on the tides, the influence of the full moon over certain individuals, and the significance of sunspots and their influence on this planet.

If the moon can affect people and entire oceans, imagine the far greater implications of the larger planets exerting their own sway on the progress of human affairs. Though a complex and highly intricate subject, astrology can thus at least begin to make sense to even the most hardened sceptic.

Though it has been around for more than 4000 years, materialistic scientists still try to malign and disparage this ancient art. Thankfully, as with other alternative and mystical practises, there has been a resurgence of interest in astrology in the past twenty-five years.

In May 2004 a bombshell book was published that offered a major boost to the quite legitimate claims of astrologers to be able to divine the future by means of computing the positions of the planets at the time of birth.

Dr. Percy Seymour, a member of Britain's Royal Astronomical Society rocked a lot of establishment boats with his work entitled: The Scientific Proof of Astrology.

He argues in the book that the relationship of the earth and everything on it, including human beings, plants, and animals, to other planets in the Solar System is very important to life here on earth. Dr. Seymour has confirmed what astrologers and psychics have been saying for centuries: that our lives are governed by a multiplicity of cosmic forces.

Apart from the positions of the Sun, Moon, and planets at birth, another factor that determines the course of our lives is the vital issue of what exactly we need to learn in a forthcoming earth life.

This depends to a large extent on how we have lived our previous lives, on what we need to LEARN in a forthcoming earth life, and, possibly, on the nature of the mission we have to accomplish here on earth.

In my own case, I believe I incarnated on earth to bring solace, consolation, and comfort to bereaved people by providing them with evidence of life after death. That was certainly a crucial part of my life-mission.

My readings have helped a lot of people find contentment and peace of mind, whether in relation to hearing from loved ones in the Spirit World, or concerning guidance in decision-making.

REINCARNATION ...
THE WHEEL OF LIFE, DEATH, AND RE-BIRTH

Mention of our actual purpose in coming to earth brings us to the subject of reincarnation. This refers to re-birth on the physical plane. It is very necessary that the human entity can have the option of returning to earth in many lives: Even the longest lifespan on earth would be far too short to facilitate one's full spiritual growth and evolution.

Reincarnation affords us all with the opportunity to achieve our goals and progress towards the attainment of those qualities of wisdom and spiritual maturity that will enable us to move on to ever higher and more refined levels of existence in the afterlife.

In readings, I can tell from the palm if a person is an old or young soul, meaning if he or she has lived many lives on earth or is a relative newcomer.

In addition to living in the Spirit World, human beings reincarnate time and again to learn certain lessons on earth. The earth plane could be compared to a school where we come to experience all that life here has to offer. Some experiences are uplifting and positive, others painful and hard to endure.

We learn from all of these experiences, each one of them adding to our store of knowledge and perception. But every aspect of living is part of the intricate fabric of existence on this earth plane.

Shakespeare said: "All the World's a Stage", and so it is: for each of us, he added, plays many parts in the long running drama of life on the earth plane.

In one incarnation, you may be poor and downtrodden, in another rich and famous-though most people find themselves somewhere in between these two extremes.

In the great earth pageant, you can be a butcher, a baker, a candle-stick maker, or find yourself in the role of any one of a thousand parts to "fill the scene" on life's eternal stage.

And the people who share this stage with us may return for future "shows" when we reincarnate on earth. A sister in one life may be a friend or business partner in the next; a man who murders a fellow human being in one life may himself come to a similar end in a future incarnation.

Or he may have to devote himself to helping victims of crime or counselling relatives of murder victims ... whatever atonement is deemed most fitting.

Every situation in life has a purpose. We are thrown together with a bewildering assortment of people, including plenty we don't like and a few we hate the sight of.

But by mixing, and interacting, with these vastly different personalities, we evolve and mature. Situations and "chance meetings" that appear accidental are seldom so: They happen for a reason.

The numbers of possible permutations are endless. Underpinning the cycle of earth lives, or birth and re-birth, is a rock sold universal law of cause and effect that ensures no person can escape the consequences of his or her actions. Good deeds are rewarded, bad or evil deeds are penalised.

Every trial or challenge that confronts us in the School of Life has a purpose, and we grow in understanding as we meet the various challenges along the way.

We are born with a "map", charting the course of the kind of life we have ahead of us. Certain lessons have to be learnt, certain tasks have to be accomplished.

One's present earth life is just one of several, part of a long cycle of existence stretching back into the remote past, and into the future. The number of earth incarnations we undergo depends on our progress.

Nobody escapes the consequences of evil deeds. Even those who have been clever enough to evade justice on earth, or who could afford a clever lawyer to get them off the hook, have to face the music at some stage in the future. Every action has to be accounted for.

In addition to being dealt with severely on the Other Side, people who commit horrible acts, such as murder, war crimes, sexual abuse, or other serious offences can find themselves back on earth paying the price of their past wrongs.

The necessity for this is obvious: A person who has committed a grievous crime on earth cannot progress beyond the lowest levels in the afterlife.

Therefore, if he is not to remain stuck in the bleak shadow lands, bemoaning his fate for eons of earth time, he must return to earth and undo the effects of his negative actions.

He can atone for his crimes through suffering on a par with that inflicted on his victims OR by becoming a crusader for justice, a tireless worker for the poor; or by dedicating himself with unswerving commitment to whatever virtuous actions or activities can best serve to expiate or make amends for his previous descent into criminality.

If he repays his debt through this follow-up life of hardship and unselfish devotion to helping his fellow human beings, he may find upon returning to the Spirit World that he has earned the right to dwell in a higher sphere than that which awaited him after his previous life of wrongdoing.

Over and over again, humans leave the Spirit World to be born again on the physical plane. They return to experience the joys and sorrows, and ups and downs of life in the School of Hard Knocks.

We find ourselves helping those we have wronged, and learning to love, or at least tolerate and accept, people we have hated, mistrusted, or despised in a previous life.

Just as an actor can play a prince one day, and a beggar the next, or change from the costume of an elegant and refined "lady of the manor" into that of a humble house maid, so also does an incarnating spirit fill vastly different roles, depending on what debts have to be paid and which lessons have to be learned.

Though we have to climb many mountains and endure much hardship along the way, we must try as best we can to live honestly, help other people, and avoid hurting even those who test our patience to the limits. When we are unkind or heartless in our dealings, we too will experience unkindness and misunderstandings at some future point in time; if not in the present life, then most certainly in another life.

Eventually, by trial and repeated error, we arrive at a perfect understanding of the law of cause and effect-of cosmic retributive justice- that governs life on earth.

Then we treat our fellow humans, as we ourselves would like to be treated in comparable circumstances. Through various lives, we experience wealth and destitution, success and failure, the intoxication of power over others and its opposite: total dependence or humiliation: an outgoing personality or an introverted one ... and so on.

All these experiences lead us to the pinnacle of spiritual adulthood. Gradually, we come to a total realisation of the Golden Rule and its supreme importance: Do unto others... as you would have them do unto you.

CHAPTER 14

Words of Comfort ... and Caution

I FIND every sitting is different, exciting, and though I am a psychic medium, I would add ... unpredictable! One never knows what family member of the sitter is going to come through. People often have the idea that they can make somebody in the Spirit World send a message to them.

They sometimes demand that such a person come through. But demands of this kind are pointless and unhelpful. One cannot force or pressurise spirits to communicate: They do so exclusively of their own free will and of their own accord.

I act as a channel for the spirits – they work through me – but I cannot command somebody's loved one to manifest at a reading, as people sometimes expect. But in most cases, a person's loved ones will come through, even if not specifically the spirit people the sitter had in mind.

Instead of a father or grandmother, for example, perhaps another relative will come through to assure the sitter that all is well on the Other Side, to pacify their grieving or concerned relatives on earth and let them know that they will see each other again in the Spirit World. I am always delighted when a sitter receives a comforting or supportive message. It is good to perceive the joy and relief this brings, the uplifting feeling that follows once the sitter knows that a loved one is at peace and healed.

It is uplifting for me too. I share the joy experienced by the person opposite me.

Sceptics ask: how can somebody know that a message comes from a person in the Spirit World, and that the message is really from the person whose name I pick up?

The answer is straightforward enough: Quite often the message contains some reference or item of personal information that could not possibly be known to myself, or indeed any other medium.

The loved one in the Spirit World may refer to a specific event or draw attention to a little known fact or humorous incident.

For example, if a reference is made to somebody's "red scarf with the blue spots on it that looked well around a blonde head", this would impress the sitter if it tallied with the sitter's knowledge of the person referred to. A simple piece of evidence can provide the confirmation of survival that a sitter needs to hear.

TRUTH HURTS!

Sometimes the TRUTH that emerges from the Other Side during a session can be dramatic and literally life changing. A person who has been in denial over any kind of personal misbehaviour or a past pivotal event concerning a loved one now in the Spirit World may be confronted with the stark reality of his actions, thoughts, decisions, or intentions when the person he wronged or took for granted comes through at a reading. The spirit person may decide to put him in the picture about the true nature of the failures or ill-conceived choices that spawned heartbreak, misunderstanding, or God only knows what consequences for other human beings.

I well remember the day a proud businessman strode into my consultation room for a reading. The session had no sooner got underway when the man's father came through and this particular occupant of the Spirit World was not exactly in the best of humour. "You did me out of everything" he accused, "You ruined the business that I built up with all that hard work. You laid it in ruins!"

His son was flabbergasted. Shock and surprise turned to remorse as the impact and shattering moral significance of this communication sunk in. He broke down, crying. Regaining his composure, he promised his father, and himself, that he would mend his ways. He promised to end the "trickery and deceit".

He explained that he had squandered and whittled away most of the business bequeathed to him by his father. He had broken the man's heart. Looking on from the Spirit World, his father was aware of the bad turn events in the family business had taken, not just in the final years of his earthly life, but also in the time that had elapsed since his arrival on the Other Side.

I cannot overstate the enormity of the impact such a message from the Spirit World can have on somebody still coping with the slings and arrows of life on earth.

It can certainly have a beneficial effect. Like Paul on the road to Damascus, a person who sees the error of his or her ways during a sitting may amend that "wrong turning" on the road of life and get back on track.

None of us is perfect. We all make mistakes, bad judgements, and crazy decisions. We say and do things that cause immense hurt, though we may not have intended such consequences.

Somebody who has reached that "other shore" after leaving behind the earth plane can help us to see life's challenges in a new perspective. They speak with authority. They have reviewed their own lives and have been shown where they erred or failed in their earthly sojourns.

With the benefit of real insight and wisdom, they can help us to avoid the pitfalls and offer a guiding word or two to us, their loved ones on this side of the cosmic great divide that appears to separate our world from the world of spirit.

I say "APPEARS" because the apparent gulf can be bridged by a thought or a whisper to those people who have gone out of our lives for a while ... but who will meet us again when we cross over to that wonderful state of being that awaits us at the end of life's long adventure.

The advice and warning received by the businessman from his father was not to his liking-but he needed to hear it. It was a shock to the system that he needed to re-direct and reconstruct his disastrous career.

We can all do with a bit of telling-off occasionally. Wasn't it the great man himself who said: "The TRUTH will set you free"?

LETTING GO AND MOVING ON

When people go to the Spirit World, they want their friends and relatives back on earth to love again, and enjoy full, meaningful relationships. They don't wish them to live isolated, lonely lives on the earth plane, but to MOVE ON and be happy.

This is important to remember because so many bereaved people are reluctant to let go, and may retreat from life, refusing to get into another relationship out of loyalty to a departed loved one.

While it is good to nurture memories of our loved ones who have passed over, we are not rewarding or satisfying them by using our love for them to hold us back.

They are conscious, and so can we be, of the glorious re-union in the Spirit World that awaits all of us when we meet them again. In the meantime, earthly life must go on. Our spirit people will be happy to see us overcome grief and sorrow occasioned by their passing.

They want us to go on to make new friends and form new, fulfilling relationships. We are entitled to seek happiness in the world. It is our birthright.

ROADSIDE MEMORIALS

On the other side of the coin, we owe it to our loved ones who have crossed over to mark their transition from this world with dignity and due reverence.

A gravestone in a cemetery, or a suitable memorial plaque in the case of cremation, is perfectly adequate, though it is nice also to read anniversary notices in the local newspapers that do homage to these people who were and are so close to us and that we have never stopped loving or caring about.

This brings me to another form of remembrance that people may feel is necessary in some cases of bereavement. Driving through Ireland, you will have noticed quite a few memorial stones erected along roadsides.

These can be seen at the sites of tragic accidents, and one can empathise with the need felt by families of crash victims to mark the spot where their loved one made his or her exit from the earth plane.

I want to assure you that there is no need, or obligation, to erect such roadside memorials. Your loved one is quite content with having his or her name etched on a gravestone, in a place of peace and tranquillity that people can visit. They want you to get on with your own life.

Though the prevalence of roadside memorials is understandable, the spirit people have no need of such "markers" and are perfectly happy to be remembered in the traditional graveyard setting. Headstones, of whatever shape, size or appearance, belong in a cemetery.

Just as they wish us to get on with our lives, we too should respect their right to move on. It is good to remember them ... but in a way they would have wanted.

WHAT I CAN'T REVEAL IN READINGS

When doing a reading, I have to be tactful as well as helpful and informative. There are often painful details relating to a sitter's life situation or that of his or her family that become known to me and that I just cannot reveal to them because of the effect I know this information would have on the person.

I see the most shocking images of betrayal, criminal activity, and aggressive behaviour that I cannot reveal to a sitter, owing to the obvious sensitivities involved.

No purpose would be served by laying bare such negative or self-destructive activities, though I can draw attention in a careful, non-judgemental way to what is revealed to me.

There is also the factor of free will. Just as people in the Spirit World offer healing, advice, and inspiration, but never compel us to change direction, so too do I refrain from pressurising any person to follow a specific course of action.

I can only help to point the way. There are certain future probabilities that could, if revealed, exercise an undue influence over decision making. We all need to learn certain lessons and undergo particular experiences in our lives.

It may be better for some people to learn from mistakes and "wrong turns" on the road of life than to consciously avoid hurdles that need to be overcome.

Occasionally, a medium or other psychic may be asked to yield damaging information on someone's enemies, business partners, spouses, lovers, or other people.

You might get a request like: "here's a picture of the staff at the office, tell me who's loyal and who's not to up scratch". Or a husband might wish to know if his wife is faithful, or whom she's been seeing.

I refrain from providing such information, or sharing any knowledge that could be used for unethical or hurtful purposes.

One has an obligation to use a psychic gift wisely, to bear in mind that free will reigns supreme on the earth plane.

To give somebody an "edge" over another person by passing on highly sensitive information that might wreak havoc in other people's lives would be irresponsible and unethical.

Black magic is another matter. There are people in the world who operate on the dark side, using paranormal forces and energies to defeat opponents, enemies, and rivals. Such activity is dangerous, not only to those who fall victim to it, but also, potentially, to the practitioners of black magic: If they do harm to another human being, this may rebound on themselves, returning with a vengeance to punish them for their misdeeds.

There are things I prefer not to be shown, and there are situations and scenarios that become known to me during a reading that I have to be careful about revealing to sitters.

Because every human being has free will, there can never be any question of spirit people compelling or pressuring earthly people into changing direction in their lives, or avoiding future situations, even if these are fraught with danger.

Any psychic will have to be tactful also in dealing with family situations that come to light. Many of these involve delicate decisions and moral balancing acts.

Of course, happy and life-enhancing moments or developments require no such scrupulous agonising: I remember when my daughter was having her third child in England. The baby wasn't due for a month.

I was in the kitchen at home when my spirit guide informed me that it would be a baby girl. I went to the phone under a kind of spell and rang my daughter.

I told her she would have the baby at the weekend. "So what I am going to have?" she asked. I said "Tell your husband to call me after the birth and I'll tell him personally".

She had the baby at the weekend and their husband, over the phone, asked me to tell him if the child were a boy or a girl. "A baby girl of course", I said confidently. Mother and baby were in the best of health.

On other occasions, I predicted wins at bingo for my daughter. She had happily told her friends of the predictions beforehand, and they were suitably impressed with the outcome!

MONEY AND WILLS

Speaking of money ... some people are so attached to their material wealth that when they cross over they want to take it with them.

As money has no value in the Spirit World, it is pointless wishing to cling on to it.

I have experienced readings for people where spirits came through demanding their money! The person might say something like: "What have you done with all my money ... you've been spending it on me. I want it back".

I explain to these spirit people that they have no need of money at this stage, and that it is right and proper that those left behind are free to enjoy it.

They remain silent or a bit grumpy for a few moments, but then gradually accept their situation and acknowledge that their families should enjoy, and get the best from, this material wealth, which is of course unnecessary in the Spirit World where no currency is required and nothing has to be paid for with money.

Spirits who feel guilty about having bequeathed money or property to people outside the family, or who have left their families in dire straits by leaving them nothing, often come through at readings to express remorse and apologise.

They wish they could change their decision, but they can't- the legal papers have all been signed so the damage has been done.

Many families have been left penniless. Begrudging or just plain nasty minded people decide to deny an inheritance to them and the benefits go elsewhere. Such unwise and conniving individuals have to face up to their moral blindness and lack of responsibility.

The Higher Spirit shows them how their heartless decision has impacted on those affected by it. Whenever I happen to meet this type of person here on the earth plane-while there is yet time to change the will- I remind them that money doesn't buy up the golden seats in Heaven. You cannot take a single coin or bank note across the Great Divide.

From the Other Side, spirits can see their former wealth, property, or other possessions being "drunk" away or otherwise squandered by the people they left it to. They come back at readings in an effort to make amends to their loved ones.

They may or may not be forgiven, depending on the person who has been on the receiving end of their stinginess.

CONJUGAL VISITS?

Not only can occupants of the Spirit World make contact with us. Many people report having experienced various forms of sexual encounters with them!

The loss of a partner who was dearly loved is felt on more than one level. As well as missing his or her company, the bereaved person will naturally yearn for those nights of passion that spiced up the relationship.

Some people can enter a trance, or get out of their physical bodies during meditation or what is termed an "altered state of consciousness" with a view to meeting someone they loved who has crossed over.

The flame of passion is re-ignited when long separated lovers meet again. They embrace in the throes of sexual desire on the plane of existence that lies between our earth and the Spirit World.

People have described such experiences to me over the years. It is only right and just that people can, in certain circumstances; avail of such "conjugal visits" by their lovers.

ANNIVERSARIES

Spirit people tend to come back to the earth plane for anniversaries or special occasions such as weddings, christenings, or funerals.

They gather unseen at these events, perhaps to lend moral support, or if necessary, healing to relatives. Afterwards, they return to the Spirit World.

Without thinking about it, people at these functions make speeches in which they say that so-and-so is "with us today in spirit". In fact, the person referred to is likely to be present, observing the proceedings and wishing everybody well.

While out driving, I occasionally notice one or more of them sitting beside me or in the back seats of the car. They stay for a while and get out of the car at some point along the journey.

One day, I had people travelling with me and they were mortified when I remarked that I had invisible passengers. I got a ferocious smell of drink from these spirit people.

They were quite merry, indicating that they had celebrated in style whatever events drew them back to the earth plane. My grandson in the car was a bit apprehensive about sharing the space with our guests! The inebriated lads were still in great form when they got off on the road to Graiguenamanagh.

Speaking of drink, I should mention that some earthbound spirits are people who were so fond of the pub on earth that they simply refuse to move on after death. Instead of progressing in the Spirit World, they prefer to hang around the earth plane for a while, imbibing the fumes of alcohol.

The pub may have been so central a part of their social lives and the drink so dear to them that they continue to feel drawn to the old haunts they loved so well. They may try to speak to drinking pals at the counter, but of course the lads can't hear them.

Eventually, such people tire of this loitering on the earth plane and feel a desire to move on. They decide to continue with their advancement and spiritual evolution on the Other Side. It's a question of them adjusting to the greater reality of life beyond the physical world.

Once the spirit opens his mind to the need to vacate the earth plane, compassion and

understanding greet his request and he can then embrace the true joys of the afterlife.

IN YOUR DREAMS ...

A safe way for non-psychics to make contact with loved ones is to meet them in dreams. In dreams, we often leave our bodies and meet our loved ones "half-way". They come closer to the earth plane and we approach nearer to their level of existence. When you wake with a memory of having seen or spoken to somebody in a dream, it may be that you really have encountered that person.

If the dream has left a deep impression, and seemed more vivid and real than the average dream, then this increases the possibility that you have indeed met your friend or relative from the Spirit World. If you wish to meet a loved one in a dream, resolve to yourself before you go asleep that you will see him or her.

Repeat your wish to yourself a number of times. Upon awakening, if you have a clear recollection of a meeting, a good idea is to write down a few details of your encounter immediately.

Keep a pen and paper by your bedside for this purpose. The reason is that the dream memory fades quickly ... so reach for the pen once you wake up and set down what happened before these precious and elusive images evaporate like the morning mist.

The temptation is to go back to sleep and hope you'll remember it later. But it's better to record your experience while it is still fresh in your mind.

If you have a clear memory upon awaking that you have met a departed loved one, what has probably happened is that you and he/she have come together on one of the spirit planes close to the earth world.

The more vivid the colours associated with the dream, and the greater the overall emotional impact of the experience, the more likely it is that it was an encounter with the person you had in mind.

Throughout history, people have reported visitations in dreams from people who had passed over. Sometimes, a person appears in the dream to reassure the dreamer that a loved one is now safe and well on the Other Side. Or somebody may warn of a future disaster that can be avoided. You can dream in pictures or in symbols. Some dreams are not to be taken too literally. Instead, they need to be deciphered and interpreted as they may convey meanings that at first seem unclear. You need to reflect on your dreams, and learn from them. However, as with Tarot readings, do not become enslaved by these nocturnal experiences. They can guide, and offer occasional insights ... but you must never let them rule your life or cloud your judgement.

CHAPTER 15

Religion should Heal ... not Hurt

O FTEN I am asked if I am a Catholic or if I believe in God. I am proud to say that I was brought up as a Catholic and that I have always believed in God.

My awareness, through first hand psychic knowledge of other spiritual dimensions, of the FACT that we survive physical death, means that I do not have to assume God's existence as a matter of faith. I am in the privileged position of knowing with absolute certainly that God-the Higher Spirit-watches over all of us in his creation.

Unfortunately, I have also experienced the negative side of religion: the heartache and cruel misunderstandings caused by official Church rules that were enacted, not by God, but by misguided human beings motivated by some very strange notions of morality and of what constitutes "proper behaviour".

I have always loved and respected the solemn rituals of the Catholic Church, the feeling of blessed peace and tranquillity that fills the interior of all places of worship, from the smallest country chapel to the rich towering cathedrals of the world.

I remember as a child fasting from seven o clock in the morning for Sunday mass.

We couldn't let a morsel of food pass our lips. To receive Communion without fasting was considered a major sin. The

Catholic Church was all-powerful in my young days, and well into my adult life.

After my marriage ended, I came face to face with the downside of Catholicism – its narrow and ill-conceived bigotry in the sphere of human relationships. The marriage had lasted twenty years, and once it was over I formed another relationship.

This news was not well received in the confession box. I tried to explain to a priest that I had found love again after a failed marriage. He leaned heavily on the chapter and verse of church doctrine and official dogma.

He denied me absolution on the grounds that, according to Catholic teaching, I was "living in sin".

But without batting an eyelid, he added that I should of course continue to rear my children in the One, True, and Apostolic Faith, and see that they went to mass. But the Sacraments were not for "sinners" like me. I was really taken aback by the sheer hypocrisy of this advice.

I was being told, in effect, that I was not good enough to receive the Sacraments, but the Church expected me to bring up my children in the Catholic faith. And all because a marriage had ended!

Repulsed by this attitude, I went to three other priests, and they too refused absolution. Incredible though it may seem, the church's attitude to marriage break-up was that "you made your bed, so lie in it". If your marriage was on the rocks, tough luck, but don't even think about loving again!

To be fair, I did in later years find a priest who granted me absolution. Times changed, and the supposedly unchangeable rules were either relaxed or quietly set aside to cater for an evolving and maturing society.

Thankfully, nowadays this whole issue of second relationships doesn't bother most people: They just carry on living and loving and pay scant regard to what the Church says.

Sadly, a lot of women were turned off the Church and alienated from its teachings by "moral policing" and degradation. In my own case, while I remained a Catholic, I pulled away from regular Mass attendance.

Today, I visit a church mainly for christenings, weddings, communion or confirmation, and funerals. But I continue to pray. Because of my psychic gifts I realise how precious these quiet chats with God, our creator, can be.

Another church teaching that caused a lot of distress was the one on Limbo. According to this atrocious doctrine, babies who died without being baptised were barred from entering Heaven. But neither would they go to Hell or Purgatory, the priests maintained, as they were innocent of any crime.

So instead, said the church, the babies that lacked the Sacrament of Baptism had to spend eternity in a place called Limbo, a gloomy state of being somewhere between the other afterlife locations where they existed forever in a state of total uncertainty, separate from their parents and loved ones.

This teaching had no basis in fact and is now seldom referred to by the church, despite being a memorable and acknowledged facet of Irish Catholicism. The Church has never officially "dropped" a belief in Limbo from its instruction, and has yet to apologise to families for the anxiety and trauma that must have resulted from such a mixed-up crazy teaching.

One can only imagine what suffering mothers went through after hearing that their children may have ended up in a dismal or featureless afterlife scenario – as if a just and merciful God would condemn them to such a fate.

From my direct experience and perception of the Spirit World, and knowledge of the afterlife state, I can confirm that Limbo is A MYTH. Babies or children that cross over, whether they have been baptised or not, are well cared for on the Other Side.

As I've already stated, they grow to maturity in a loving, caring environment and get to meet loved ones in the Spirit World.

Like the teaching about fiery devils prodding people with pitchforks, the Limbo myth was conjured up out of fertile or overactive imaginations to gain power over mass-goers.

The fact that Limbo is seldom if ever mentioned nowadays has caused people to ask if the church itself even believed in it, and to wonder about its motives in ever formulating such a heartless doctrine. One way or the other, there is no need to worry about it.

Limbo is a figment of fantasy, a fictitious place invented by misguided men who perhaps thought it would frighten parents into baptising children. I repeat: For babies there is only compassion and a joyful existence in the Spirit World. Those who have lost children may rest assured on that.

While paying due reverence to Catholicism, I want to emphasise that I respect all religious belief. When we cross over, God is there for us. The colour of our skin, and the brand of religious conviction-or lack of it- to which we subscribe in earthly life are totally irrelevant.

The various creeds and religions of the world are different roads leading to God. Nobody is excluded from the afterlife. All arrivals are welcomed with open arms regardless of their individual beliefs.

MANY MANSIONS

There are "many mansions" in Heaven, and people inhabit whichever zone or level is appropriate to their outlook or belief or point of spiritual evolution. People of a stronger belief, such as priests, nuns, bishops, mystics, etc tend to gravitate towards a different level than those with a lesser degree of faith or interest in theological matters.

You might say that, in a sense, we all occupy our own "little heavens" within the Spirit World. The realms of spirit are dotted with places of worship to cater for all religious affiliations.

The scenic beauty of the "other-worldly" landscape is enhanced and complemented by these symbols of faith, hope, and devotion that mean so much to the majority of earth's inhabitants.

But on the Other Side they co-exist in complete harmony, each religion or set of beliefs having its own "space" in which to comfort followers and exert a positive healing influence. How different from conditions on the earth plane where disagreements over religion have spawned wars and massacres, bitterness and division, fear and loathing, throughout history.

The downside side of religion, as experienced on earth, gives way to tolerance and spiritual maturity on the Other Side. Catholics can go to Mass if they wish, Moslems can enter mosques; and there are synagogues for the Jews.

Likewise, Hindus, Buddhists, Sikhs, Jehovah's Witnesses, and adherents of every other creed, sect, or belief system in this world can exercise their religious freedom without the slightest impediment. Variety is the spice of life Over There. It is only on earth that religious or sectarian bigotry or censorship prevents people from giving proper expression to their beliefs.

To a considerable extent, we create the conditions we meet after death by our actions during earthly life. Somebody who commits a brutal rape, murder, or war crime will occupy a lower level of existence than a person who has led a decent life free of such outrages.

Our personal likes and dislikes are reflected there too. If we prefer to live in a bungalow than in a mansion or a lush apartment, this preference will be catered for in the Spirit World. We can have the kind of home we choose, and whatever furnishings we deem apt.

People who on earth have loved gardening can bask in the glory of a florist's dream come true, surrounded by glowing or exotic foliage exhibiting splashes of soothing, brilliant colour. Though we don't need to eat in the Spirit World, we can if we want to. There are no limits placed on the amount or variety of food available to us.

As a rule, newcomers opt to dine as they did while on earth. Spirits who came through at sèances over the decades have spoken of drinking endless cups of tea and having anything they desired in the line of food. But as they advanced and evolved spiritually, they found that food was not a necessity-that eating was a habit carried over from the earth plane that could be freely exercised ... but dispensed with at any point. I deal with these tantalising issues of food and housing elsewhere in the book.

People progress at their own pace in the Spirit World. Education, learning, and advancement are integral to our lives over there.

I have seen the breathtakingly beautiful landscapes, the green fields, towering mountain ranges, the tranquil blue skies, the flowers, the trees, the lakes, the exotic wildlife, and the great Halls of Learning. No words we use on earth can adequately describe the loveliness of the Spirit World's topography or its divine aesthetic appeal.

Heaven is the Other Side of the physical world. It is, I have discovered, similar in many ways to this earth. Apart from living in houses, we can and do learn and further our education in a variety of ways. Learning is important, and we all progress at our own pace in the Spirit World.

If we have failed to achieve certain goals on earth, we can, in many cases, achieve these on the Other Side. In the Spirit World, children who pass over can attend school, to be educated by the Higher Spirits. I have been allowed to see this wonderful process.

But there is one practise common to earthly life that has no place in the Spirit World. That is use of wealth or money to advance one's position or to gain social or material advantage.

I remember how in Graiguenamanagh of my youth, some of the pews in the church had names inscribed on them. Families in the area had bought these, and each family had its own private seating.

Anyone sitting in Mr. so-and so's section of the church would quickly realise his or her mistake. This was a form of snobbery, and of course nobody will ever be judged by God on the basis of what part of a church they sat in.

Unfortunately, many people have a similar attitude to "securing their place" in the next life. They think they can buy up the best seats in Heaven by flashing money around.

In the past, the system of "indulgences" brought the church into disrepute. It was believed that the more money you paid in envelopes, or put in the collection boxes, the greater your chances of occupying one of the Golden Seats in Heaven.

Or you could supposedly get a few months or years off your "sentence" in Purgatory by making a large donation to a bishop or priest.

In reality, money ceases to have any value once you pass through the gates of death into the spirit world. You leave behind material wealth but you take with you the consequences of all the good or bad deeds of your life, and the fruits of your achievements on earth, as well as your memories, acquired knowledge and wisdom, and the talents you developed.

That is why we should heed the advice which is common to all religions, regardless of how backward they might be in other respects: To reject evil thought and actions, and to make your life, as far as possible, one that you can look back on with joy and satisfaction when you reach the Other Side.

When you think you of it, this is just a common sense outlook. By going good, and avoiding the infliction of pain and suffering on others, you gain happiness, peace of mind, and you can be sure of ascending to the higher realms of spirit.

The road to spiritual maturity may be long and strewn with both obvious and hidden pitfalls. Temptation is never too far away. Negative or evil influences abound along the Highway to Heaven, each and every one of them a challenge to our ability to cope with, and overcome them.

But the rewards are great for all who refrain from dark deeds and hateful thoughts: And greater still for those who pursue virtuous, caring, unselfish lives.

The humble Buddhist or Christian monk who devotes his life to good works, though he may not have a penny to his name, is of a higher spiritual order than a well heeled super rich tycoon who spends money as if it grew on trees and lives a life of care-free opulence.

Most of us are somewhere in between these two polar opposites. Not terribly bad or nasty individuals, but not exactly saints either. Saints are in short supply in this imperfect world of ours, but there are lots of caring people who work day in and day out to make the world a better, fairer, healthier, less threatening, more tolerant place in which to live.

Some of them we never even hear about. They work quietly, behind the scenes, chipping away at poverty, injustice, inequality, or helping victims of sexual abuse and the various other unspeakable crimes committed by humans on this earth.

As mentioned before, the earth plane could be likened to a school. We enter it at birth and say goodbye to it after death, having learned whatever lessons we agreed on prior to our present incarnation. It was never going to be easy, but how exhilarating to meet and then overcome even the stiffest of those challenges!

There is much hype and controversy these days about the nature of various school exams: Are they fair or not? Are students pressurised too much? Should the structure of the exam system be changed? And so on.

But we sometimes fail to focus on the biggest test of all: the one we undertake when we opt to be born on Old Mother Earth. We don't sit that exam on a sweltering day in June. We face it every day in the ups and downs of just being human. We'll know for certain how we've fared when the bells of Heaven go ding-a-ling-ling to call us back to our Home in the Spirit World.

Once we do our best in the context of our life plan, we'll have passed the gruelling test with flying colours.

CHAPTER 16

Good News for Animal Lovers!

PEOPLE WHO come for readings often raise the question of animals in the afterlife. They wonder if they will ever again see their beloved pets that have died. I can reassure you all on that point. I know from what I have seen, and been told by spirit beings, that you will be re-united with your pets ... they live on in the Spirit World.

Remember the Irish ballad that went: "sure when you go to Heaven ... you can bet your dollar note ... that the angel with the whiskers is Paddy McGinty's Goat ...".

That crazy old song wasn't too far off the mark!

Spirits who communicated through the English direct voice medium, Leslie Flint, spoke of their joy upon discovering that their long dead pets were alive and well on the Other Side. A rag and bone merchant described how he entered the Spirit World, worrying that he would have to meet his two wives, neither of whom he liked very much.

Michelle, Moira's daughter, celebrating Foxy's 8th birthday.

Instead, his faithful horse, Jenny, for whom he had great affection, greeted him. She had been closer to him than any woman; he told people gathered at the sèance.

Not only that. This man recounted how when he awoke in what seemed like a hospital in the Spirit World, he later found himself in a field, sitting under a tree. It was a perfect setting for his reunion with the old horse. An even greater surprise followed when the horse actually spoke to him, by telepathy.

Then he realised that the animal, and indeed all animals, have a special purpose on earth and deserved to be treated properly, as he had treated Jenny.

Another spirit, also communicating through Mr. Flint, recalled his astonishment when a friendly cat turned up in the spirit world. He had just been introduced to his new home in "Heaven" and was looking around the attractive dwelling place.

The sight of a black cat sitting on a chair surprised him, as he didn't expect that animals could survive death. But then he almost dropped with the fright: The cat jumped off the chair, walked over to him and asked: "how are you?"

The man's guide in the Spirit World explained to him that cats are highly intelligent creatures but have different ways of making themselves understood than we humans have. Once in the Spirit World, cats and humans can happily communicate by thought.

Cattle, sheep, ducks or whatever takes their fancy on the other side can surround farmers who have been particularly attached to their livestock. They can dwell in the midst of beautiful pasturelands if they wish, whatever brought peace of mind and contentment on earth.

Even on earth, animals can pick up our thoughts and are sensitive to the presence of spirit beings in a house. But they really come into their own when they cross over. My mother, who was 85 when she died, brings along her pure bred Pomeranian with her sometimes when she appears to me. Pets abound in the Spirit World. Animals provide companionship on earth to countless people.

Often, the cat or dog at the fireside is the only friend an elderly person can call upon to ease the pain of loneliness.

Animals can of course prove more loyal and trustworthy than humans, as they never betray you and seek only a little affection and looking after in return for the love and loyalty they show us.

What a relief it is then for people who loved, or were dependent on them, to discover that their trusty four-legged friends live on, ready to greet them as on many a happy day back on earth.

In my own case, people have asked me a thousand times why I keep my dog "Foxy" – who was stuffed after he died – in the house. It's because I was so attached to him in life, so I liked the idea of preserving his memory.

After he passed away, I brought his mortal remains to a taxidermist. I was determined to pay this little tribute to a dog that had won his way into my heart.

I treasure his memory: He won all around him at dog shows. My loft is full to overflowing of trophies and rosettes that he took with ease when he walked tall among the best canines in the land. He turned a lot of heads in his time.

Foxy and family: Foxy was married to his sweetheart, "Star", at a cermony in Moira's garden. Beside Moira is her daughter, Saberina.

When I went shopping, he used to settle himself in the trolley, and he sulked if he thought I might leave the house without him.

When I was laid up in hospital, a relative brought him into the ward concealed in a holdall. When the coast was clear, my friend unzipped the bag and Foxy ventured his little head out to give me a kiss. He was clever enough to keep quiet until he was safely outside the hospital.

Since his death, Foxy has visited me occasionally. One night, his spirit came to my bedroom and he appeared as solid to me as when he was in his mortal body. I patted him on the head. He had come for a particular reason: It was the anniversary of his death.

When I leave my physical body at the end of life's journey, I want Foxy's earthly shell put into the coffin too. I'll be able to meet the real Foxy in the Spirit World, where he is quite content at the moment, waiting patiently for me.

Another extraordinary example of non-human intelligence is the annual visitation of a robin to my home in Bennettsbridge.

There are many superstitious folk who fear the robin as a symbol of bad luck or tragedy. But the feathered friend that flutters into my house every May is always welcome. She has visited annually since my mother died, and the bird has never missed a summer since the day of her passing.

My mother had a love of birds, and they returned her affection for them on the day of her funeral: Robins, thrushes and other winged messengers lined the walls of the graveyard as her body was laid to rest. People who gathered for the burial were dumbfounded by the spectacle: The birds had flown and fluttered from all points of the compass to be present, as if to say goodbye to their long-time friend and ally. It was a fitting, and deeply moving send-off, a guard of honour provided by the birds of the air for a gentle lady who looked after them.

The robin redbreast is a familiar sight at my home every summer. She returns with her young to visit me, heedless of the Pomeranian, or any humans who happen to be around. She knows she is among friends and therefore has no fear.

Apart from pets, wild and exotic animals have a place in the afterlife. But they co-exist in total harmony. Lions and tigers are as tame as kittens. Creatures that we consider predators on earth respect their "prey" on the other side. Their predatory instincts are no longer necessary in their new, unthreatening environment.

You won't find dogs chasing cats, hounds chasing foxes, or lions tearing strips off giraffes when you survey the idyllic spirit countryside. They have no need to misbehave or hunt for food.

Like humans, they can absorb all the sustenance they require from the etheric atmosphere. The saying that "nature is red in tooth and claw" applies only on the physical plane!

Life on earth brings out the best and the worst in all species. Humans and animals alike are engaged in a marathon struggle for existence on this planet, learning and evolving in a thousand different ways in the great School of Life.

But they – and us – will find peace once we get away from the false values, base and destructive impulses, and dire cruelties of the earth plane.

As the song says: "All God's Creatures have a Place in the Choir".

The author, holding a preserved "Foxy", whose spirit lives on and guards her home.

CHAPTER 17

Tarot and Crystal Ball: Mystical Guides to the Past, Present, and Future

I N MY readings, I use the Tarot, in addition to the crystal and the ancient art of palmistry. The Tarot is a deck of 78 cards that can be used to gain considerable insight into the problems, dilemmas, or difficult decisions facing any human being.

When read by a genuine psychic, a Tarot spread can offer strong indications of future events or probabilities.

The origin of Tarot Cards is shrouded in mystical tales of wonder and the powers of prophesy. High Priests of the declining empire of ancient Egypt devised an ingenious way of preserving the spiritual wisdom and great knowledge of the hidden worlds by condensing it all and encapsulating it in a pack of seventy-eight cards.

These would contain vast reservoirs of knowledge of the Unseen Worlds, the human spirit ... and even hold the key to the future of nations and individuals.

But this store of priceless information was hidden away amid the carefully chosen symbols, each invested with powerful imagery that would strike a chord with the unconscious minds of people.

From Egypt, the Tarot found it way to Asia, and the cards are believed to have been introduced into Europe by returning crusaders and by gypsies from India who roamed the Near East before reaching our neck of the woods.

Some of Moira's grandchildren.

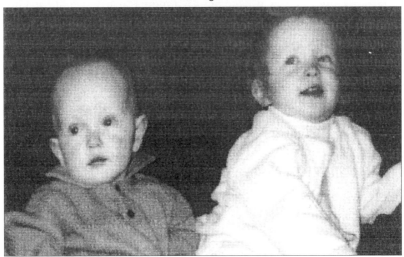

The Tarot deck comprises the Minor Arcana (56 suit cards) and the Major Arcana, or trumps ... pictorial symbol cards.

The Minor Arcana bears comparison with ordinary playing cards: There are suits of wands- corresponding to clubs. The cups in Tarot are equivalent to hearts; the swords to spades, and pentacles to diamonds.

Each suit encompasses the Court Cards familiar to mainstream card playing: kings, queens, knights, and pages.

The cards of the Major Arcana are deeply symbolic picture cards. Each of these images has a powerful meaning that immediately resonates with the psychic who does the reading.

The way the cards are laid out will depend on the individual reader and the method or approach that works best for her.

The entire pack can be used in a reading, or just the Major Arcana. Apart from the cards that show up in a spread, the relationship of each card to the others can also have significance, depending on the style or personality of the reader.

Among the possible Tarot configurations employed are the three-card spread for concise reading, the Celtic Cross layout, and a Horoscope spread based on astrology.

I use the Tarot to unlock the secrets of the human mind and to open pathways to the future. In so doing, I strive to help people find happiness and the fulfilment that is every person's birthright. If you seek a loving relationship, for example, the cards can show where, how, and possibly when love may enter your life.

Such advice can be of enormous benefit ... if rendered cautiously, with due tact and sensitivity. The cards reveal surprises that lay in store ... the engagement rings, the weddings, the happy gatherings, perhaps the arrival of babies ... all the heart stopping milestones along the emotional roller coaster that is the path of true love and romance.

The Tarot is rich in symbolism, and these time-honoured symbols will help to point towards potential or likely careers and life changing events or circumstances. They also warn of betrayals: Forewarned is forearmed.

The symbols of the Tarot can sound warnings also of disasters ahead, and indicate how best to either avoid these, or at least how one might cope with and weather the storm of these bad patches that all of us have to face in life.

In theory, anyone can do a Tarot reading, but a psychic has an advantage when it comes to interpreting the spreads and layouts. Equally important, he or she can attune to the energies surrounding the person for whom the reading is provided.

I always ask the sitter to pick the cards so that his/her energies and personal vibration can enter the equation.

At readings, I am aware also of spirit energies in the room. So I can combine my other psychic perceptions with the power of the Tarot to elicit information or advice that may be of use to the person sitting opposite.

A word of caution to people who either use the Tarot themselves or seek regular readings from psychics or non-psychics: The Tarot cannot be considered infallible, but more as a guide to the future. As stated elsewhere in the book, the future is not written in stone.

Though pathways can be charted, it is up to the individual whether to tread these or instead to change course and veer off in another direction. Free will is the factor that can nullify the predictions of even the greatest Tarot readers.

The Tarot offers indications and insights, and can point to possible or probable outcomes in various life situations.

It would be a mistake, though, to live blindly by the Tarot, or to adopt a fatalistic dependence on what the cards appear to be saying. I know of people who have been frightened out of their wits by Tarot readers who told them scare stories.

They panicked when a psychic predicted imminent death, or warned that a close family member would commit suicide. These so-called Tarot readers are misusing a great force for good, turning it into a "power tool" to make themselves feel important.

In the same way that we would not wish our doctor to scare us out of our wits with over the top predictions of doom and gloom, we have a right to expect Tarot readers to act responsibly and to treat their clients with absolute respect at all times.

Tactless or unethical use of the tarot is unwarranted and unacceptable. The Death Card, for instance, might give rise to fear when it comes up in a particular configuration, prompting some people to conclude that their time on earth is drawing to a close.

In fact, the same card can indicate a change of direction in life, or the "death" of one phase of a specific undertaking or career or habit in preparation for the opening up of another chapter of life.

Be wary also of some of those Internet Tarot readings that may be just "canned" and mass-produced for public consumption. Computer generated "readings" cannot possibly have the same value as those that proceed from a face-to-face consultation.

The personal factor is missing, and a machine is simply churning out reams of garbled messages that can have little true meaning but could be dangerous if they contain prophesies of doom or alarmist messages that cause distress to sensitive or unbalanced people.

You will know the good Tarot readers because their reputations tend to precede them. You are more likely to hear of their positive and accurate readings by word of mouth.

I devote a whole chapter of this book to the hurt caused by frauds and chancers. Its inclusion was necessary, if regrettable, in view of the widespread abuse of the psychic realm by a heartless minority.

Crystal ... The art of practise of gaining knowledge of the past, present, or future by gazing into a crystal ball is called scrying. The crystal is generally made of quartz. It may be translucent or transparent, or coloured blue, white, green, or yellow.

Crystal gazing is a timeless art, dating from the ancient Persian, Egyptian, and Chinese civilisations. Other reflecting surfaces can also serve this purpose, like mirrors or pools of water. The witch in the Snow White story looks into a mirror and asks who is the fairest woman in the kingdom. This was scrying: If she were clairvoyant, she would expect the mirror to answer her tantalising question. Like so many of the old fairy tales, this part of the story was inspired by a very real psychic gift.

I use a crystal in my readings. It focuses my psychic vision. Images unfold before me like televised pictures, showing me highlights of a spirit person's earth life, or scenes from the future life of someone who has come for a reading.

Future events reveal themselves on the right of the ball, and the past appears on the left.

As with any form of psychic work, tact and compassion are essential when offering advice based on the use of the crystal. What you see is only part of the overall picture. How you interpret the images that appear in the crystal is equally important.

The crystal ball, like the Tarot, can unlock the secrets of the mind, and reveal future trends, and probabilities in our lives.

Bad news can be broken gently, or given in conjunction with a caution to the effect that the future has yet to unfold, and can take a different course from that indicated in the reading if the person avoids a particular unwise decision or decides on a major change of direction in his/her life.

A good psychic, whether he or she works with Tarot, Crystal, Palmistry, or any of the forms of divination or spiritual counselling, is there to HELP, not to frighten you half to death!

Enjoy any readings you receive. Benefit and learn from them. But do not be enslaved by what ought to be a helpful guide or a series of "signposts" to the future. Live your life in accordance with your own set of beliefs and principles.

Your decisions that the ones that count in the end ... having due regard to all guidance offered and the effects, positive or negative, of outside influences.

YOU are the master of your destiny.

CHAPTER 18

Frauds and Chancers

A S IN every profession and every line of work, there have always been fakes and frauds to be found posing as psychics. And also, as with all spheres of human activity, it must be remembered that some psychics are more gifted or competent than others.

Since the day the first psychic began to tune in to higher energies, and mediums began to receive messages from the Spirit World, the fraudsters also began their careers, leading people astray and using the reputations of decent people to give credence to their own cruel deceptions.

Over the centuries, they have hurt a lot of credulous people and their activities encourage the sceptics to reject ALL evidence of the paranormal. This can be very frustrating to those of us who really are psychic and do our best to use our God-given gifts for the benefit of humanity.

There is no strict set of guidelines laid down by the laws of the land to regulate how psychics conduct their affairs, so you have to exercise your own judgement as to which psychic reader is most helpful to you. As a rule, it is advisable to opt for a psychic who is experienced and comes highly recommended. You hear about the best psychics by word of mouth: These are the ones who don't even need to advertise. Their reputations precede them.

MYSTIC MOIRA

It goes without saying that someone who has years of successful practise to his or her credit is more likely to give a competent reading than somebody who is just starting out, or who is still in the early stages of developing his or her psychic powers.

This applies right across the psychic spectrum, whether you are dealing with mediumship, tarot, numerology, palm reading, or whatever.

Experience is the best teacher, as the saying goes, and it can take years, even decades, for a true psychic to develop to his or her full potential. In the same way, you would feel more comfortable being treated by a competent doctor than a first year medical student.

A medium's actual motive is important. It affects the quality and standard of readings provided. If money is the only or overriding motive, it may detract from his or her powers or even, according to some practitioners of the psychic art, create a situation where the medium tends to make contact with less spiritually evolved beings or lower entities.

While it is perfectly acceptable to make a living as a psychic, one has to be conscious at all times that the gift to communicate with the spirit world is God-given and can be taken away from any medium who misuses it or uses it for the wrong reasons or purposes. Materialism does not sit easy with spirituality.

A certain type of operator, endowed with little in the way of psychic ability, is tempted to cheat when messages don't come through and fabricate information.

This is not just dishonest – it is terribly unfair to people who may be pinning their hopes on hearing from a departed loved one.

Another point to remember: No honest or genuine psychic will attempt to frighten you with scare-mongering statements or predictions.

Instead, they will indicate possible or probable outcomes or eventualities, while stressing that the future is not written in stone and always open to change, depending on your own decisions and behaviour.

Anyone telling you that you are doomed, and that you can do nothing about it, is resorting to unnecessary and unacceptable fear tactics that should not be part of a reading.

What psychics can do is offer guidance to the best of their ability, based on the information they have gleaned from their paranormal insights and perceptions.

In my own practise, I always tape the reading and give the sitter the tape to take away with them. This is essential, as nobody can remember every detail of a reading.

The person can then listen as many times as they wish to the tape. As time passes, they can, if they wish, check the accuracy of any predictions made during a reading.

You are entitled to ask the psychic for a recording of the session. A refusal to provide you with a tape should be viewed with caution, as it may point to a lack of confidence on the part of the reader.

No genuine psychic has anything to hide, or anything to fear, from a tape-recording of a session.

It is only the frauds and charlatans that have every reason in the world to steer clear of recording their advice and readings or having these subjected to very close analysis, not just by the sitter, but possibly by that person's family and friends, and God knows who else.

Be conscious of your rights when you go for a reading. If a psychic does not offer a tape recording, you are entitled to bring along your own tape-recorder.

Feel free to ask questions of a psychic: You can inquire in advance about the cost of a reading, and then decide if the length of time allocated matches the price. Prices vary, as do the durations of readings.

A reading can last between half an hour and one and half hours, generally speaking.

Psychic hotlines present you with another predicament. There are hundreds of these, operating from many parts of the world. The business has mushroomed in recent years.

Here, you are dealing with someone you can't see, which means you have to use your own judgement and discretion if you decide to phone for a reading.

Even before considering the question of which reader you can trust, there is the burning issue of your telephone bill. The cost of these calls can exceed Two Euro per minute, and it is easy to forget about the cost as you become engrossed in the reading.

Times flies, and the person on the other end of the line is in no hurry to wind up the conversation: Understandably, because their jobs depend on keeping you talking!

Of course there are gifted and honourable psychics involved in the phone-in services. People have received excellent help and guidance from psychic hotlines. Indeed, some people may even prefer the anonymity that comes with talking to a complete stranger who cannot see them.

But inevitably non-psychics and downright frauds abound in this line of work. In America, controversy rages about the huge number of rip-offs that have characterised the psychic hotlines. Many frauds have been exposed.

People posing as psychics have brought grief and misery to vulnerable people who placed their trust in sham readings and bogus advice.

Victims of this quackery have ended up with psychiatric problems after being frightened out of their wits by alarmist and doom-laden predictions that no genuine psychic would have made over a phone-line.

There have been cases too of male tarot readers phoning back female callers and asking them out on dates: They get the phone numbers from caller IDs. People have been conned into parting with large amounts of money by unscrupulous frauds who have little or no psychic ability ... but plenty of charm and criminal dexterity.

So be sure to discriminate between the decent, honourable psychics and the rapidly growing army of chancers that are out to line their pockets at your expense.

If phoning a psychic hotline, keep an eye on the time and don't hang on to every word you hear. Above all, don't fall for any moneymaking scams.

If one of them asks you to meet him or her and part with a lot of money, just hang up or report them to the service provider.

Remember at all times that you have rights, and one of those is the right to sound and reliable psychic advice. The frauds need to be encouraged to take up a different line of work!

CHAPTER 19

The Dark Side:
Not Recommended!

I HAVE dealt with people in the course of my readings who have dabbled in the darker side of the occult or paranormal. It is very foolish to experiment with dark forces or to indulge in rituals that may attract foul or malicious entities.

These shadowy spirits attach themselves to people who foolishly or unintentionally conjure them up. Many of you will have seen The Exorcist, a terrifying film about a young girl who was troubled by dark spirits that inflicted great physical and psychological trauma.

Though the movie was just fiction, it reminded cinema goers of how dangerous and inadvisable it is to meddle in occult practises without being fully aware of the nature of the hidden dimensions that interpenetrate our own world and extend beyond it.

I see the malevolent entities that attach themselves to such misguided individuals. I have to cleanse these unfortunate people. I have had to literally beat away the dark or negative intruders from them.

I remember one woman who was afflicted by at least nine dark spirits. They had been around since her college days and she was now a middle-aged woman. These entities were ghastly and fearsome to behold. They resembled the hellish forms depicted in old picture stories of shock-horror and demonic possession.

Their faces changed constantly in appearance, each expression as grizzly and alarming as the ones preceding it. As well as seeing them, I heard their spine-tingling shrieks and howling.

I discovered that this woman had suffered from depression, always feeling down, and nothing had ever gone right for her since the day she inadvertently conjured up unclean spirits with an ouija board. I had to cleanse her of this terrible affliction.

With considerable effort, I succeeded in expelling the dark entities, pushing them out through the doorway and out of the house.

The woman later phoned me to say she felt a lot better after the cleansing, and that her health and general well being had improved. I definitely advise people not to dabble in the dark side of the paranormal.

There are negative forces in the hidden realms just waiting for gullible human beings that they can disturb and manipulate, leading to various forms of physical or mental illness.

CURSES

Curses can work like magic spells when directed against people with evil or malicious intent.

They can result in the victim being hurt or becoming ill. Throughout history, various cultures have incorporated the practise of deliberately cursing one's enemies.

One of the better-known methods of cursing involved creating an image or effigy: The effigy represented the intended victim.

Wax effigies were popular, though they were also made of clay, wood or cloth. The effigy used could be made to resemble the victim. Damaging the likeness of the person targeted might, depending on the strength of the curse, cause harm to the victim.

The effigy might be melted in a fire or stuck with sharp implements such as pins, thorns, or daggers. Rotten eggs were used too: Once a victim was identified and his or name recited, the eggs would be buried in the earth or thrown away.

The ancient Egyptians were firm believers in the powers of cursing: Tombs of the Pharaohs were protected by a powerful curse to prevent grave robbers or vandals from interfering with them.

However, it is important to remember that a curse need not involve any of these elaborate occult practises.

Any strongly felt or expressed desire to do harm to somebody can be considered a curse, and have an effect similar to that achieved by the magicians of old.

Curses come in all shapes and sizes. Every day of the week, people curse something or somebody. But some curses are stronger and more lethal than others.

The thought-projection formed by the curse may influence the person who we are annoyed or angry with, and affect him in various ways, depending on its relative strength and forcefulness.

If you hate a person with sufficient intensity, you are cursing him or her with those furious and vengeful thoughts. The curse many hurt the other person physically or emotionally, and wreak havoc in his life.

It may also rebound on you in a kind of boomerang effect, so do try to steer clear of hateful thoughts. Try not to nurse grudges or thoughts of "getting even" with people. Instead, where possible, make an effort to resolve the issues that gave rise to the misunderstanding or division.

If you are a victim of one of the more powerful curses of the kind formulated deliberately, as in witchcraft or some occult practises, you should seek the advice of a reputable psychic to counteract the negative influences. While we are entitled to defend ourselves from malicious attack, we must never instigate occult action against someone who has not targeted us. Bu if you believe yourself to the victim of either a deliberate or unconscious curse, you can take steps to protect yourself.

A final word of advice on this subject: Do not be deceived by so-called "psychics" who tell you that you have been cursed and that you must pay them vast sums of money to banish the evil influence.

There are back street or "seaside" fortune-tellers who tell people that they are under the sway of malevolent forces and that the only way you can escape this menace is to pay them a lot of money. Don't fall for such garbage.

You are the master of your own destiny. Nobody can take control of your life unless you allow them to: This applies as much to some of the fraudulent psychics who seek to prey upon the gullible as it does to people who "curse" their rivals or enemies.

COMEUPPANCE: THE DAY OF RECKONING

Staying with the Dark Side of humanity ... I emphasise throughout this book that people who commit horrific crimes on earth and somehow evade human justice will be dealt with severely on the Other Side.

Crime never really pays, no matter how tempting the short-term gains, be they financial or sensual in nature.

Anyone planning to commit crimes of violence, murder, or sexual abuse that cause untold heartbreak and suffering should remember that they will be judged harshly in the afterlife and held accountable for their actions.

This is not to be confused with the terrifying, scare-mongering notions of Hell that gave so many people sleepless nights in the days of the missioners.

Instead of thinking in terms of reward and punishment, we should focus on the different planes or levels of existence in the Spirit World. Jack the Ripper obviously would not find himself on the same level, or sharing the same locale on the Other Side as Mother Teresa or any other person who led a half decent life on earth.

The lowest level is unpleasant, darkish, and brooding; but not the place of hellish torment conjured up to frighten people over the centuries. It is rather the kind of low vibratory environment that certain types of people have created for themselves by their actions and lifestyles.

This would correspond to the somewhat crude concept of Purgatory that dominated Church teaching in the Middle Ages. The purpose of Purgatory in the old Catholic doctrines was to "purge": Hence the name given to this place of purging in the Spirit World. It is where people have to come to terms with the consequences of evil deeds committed on earth.

A sadistic murderer will occupy a level of existence that corresponds perfectly to his murderous thoughts, feelings, and actions.

He will have to face the consequences of his behaviour and he will see and experience the effects of his actions on his victims. In certain circumstances, he may have to reincarnate on earth to face a similar violent or unnatural death to the one he has inflicted.

Or he may have to return to the earth plane to atone for his deeds, perhaps by devoting himself to an unselfish life of service to victims of crime: Or by working among the poorest of the poor in some poverty-stricken country on the margins of civilisation.

But prior to re-incarnating to set right his dreadful wrongdoings, he will have to abide in a dreary world of half-light and dark brooding. The atmosphere on this level is distasteful and of a very low order. Desolation abounds.

Spirit communicators who have dwelt upon this subject refer to a kind of perpetual twilight or semi-darkness, of houses built of rotting wood, of swirling fetid black clouds through which light can never shine, and of an all-pervasive melancholy.

People who have dedicated their lives to hurting others, or fouling the universe with dark and hateful thoughts of violence, revenge, and cruelty tend to be attracted to these lower regions of the afterlife.

The duration of a newcomer's "sentence" in this unfortunate and unwholesome state of affairs will vary according to the nature and severity of his or her behaviour and negative thought-patterns. What is important to remember is that nobody can gravitate towards any of these levels who has not deserved the experience.

A person "wills" himself to whichever level, high or low, that is most appropriate to his earthly behaviour or overall performance on earth.

There, he can meet and associate with others of a similar disposition, all roaming this state of being. What he cannot do is move on to a higher plane until he has purged himself of his crimes.

The case of a brutal murderer is an extreme example, but you can take it that ALL OF US must account for our lives once we reach the Other Side. You have absolutely nothing to fear if you have acted honourably on earth and done your best to live a good life without hurting other people.

You will then be greeted by the glorious beauty that I have already seen with my Inner Eye: the sparkling waterfalls, the shimmering green parkland, the gardens, the buildings that are literally Out of this World, the flora and fauna exuding endless joy.

There are seven levels of advancement in the Spirit World. Again, please remember that those who intentionally inflict suffering on their fellow human beings must remain on the lowest level for quite a while by virtue of their own actions.

It is not a cruel God or any other divine being that put them in that predicament. They alone have gravitated towards the state of being best suited to their lifestyles and individual stage of advancement, or lack of it.

CHAPTER 20

Spiritualism: What is it?

S PIRITUALISM CAN refer to the widely held belief in life after death. But it is also the name of a religion that emerged in the middle of the 19th century.

At the around that time, sèances and other attempts to establish contact with the Spirit World became popular in America and for several decades a national movement that promoted spiritualist beliefs flourished there. A church dedicated to the principles and beliefs of spiritualism was also founded. It still has a worldwide following today.

The spiritualist movement fostered the belief – well supported by evidence – that the human personality continues to exist after death and that communication with the Spirit World is possible in certain circumstances. Mediums practised openly, not just in the big cites, but in hundreds of towns and villages across the USA.

At the sèances, remarkable demonstrations of psychic power and proof of survival were witnessed: Spirits materialised, tables moved, window shutters rattled, and trumpets hovered above the heads of people who had gathered in darkened rooms to communicate with the Other Side.

Spirits could cause rapping sounds to draw attention to their presence. Disembodied voices spoke through the trumpets and ghostly forms startled witnesses.

During the American Civil War, Abraham Lincoln attended regular sèances.

It was at one such gathering that a highly evolved spirit person urged him to end the horrible practise of slavery in the United States. He followed this very sound and humane advice and freed the slaves.

Queen Victoria employed a trance medium to make contact with her deceased husband. Her children were reared as spiritualists. And the late Queen Mother likewise called in a medium to see how her departed husband, King George VI was getting on in the Spirit World!

A Committee of the Church of England was appointed in 1937 to investigate Spiritualism. So great was the volume of evidence accumulated that the committee took two years to wade through it and assess its value.

As part of this comprehensive, wide-ranging investigation, Britain's top mediums were observed and studied as they established contact with the Spirit World.

When the marathon probe ended, seven of the ten Committee members concluded that at least some of the communications that occur at sèances or when mediums hold private sittings are the result of spirits making contact with people on earth.

Unfortunately, this finding was hushed up. The report on the investigation was stamped 'Private and Confidential' and kept safely removed from the public domain. The report was literally kept under lock and key in Lambeth Palace for almost four decades.

It was only in 1979 that the media got to hear of it and details of the study became common knowledge.

The greatest irony of this investigation is that the Archbishop of Canterbury, Dr. Cosmo Lang, who was scathing of the notion that mediums could contact the dead, later came through himself at a "direct voice" sèance.

He spoke clearly and with great authority in the presence of witnesses and his message was tape-recorded.

From his new stately home on the Other Side, Dr. Lang praised the efforts of mediums and admitted that he had changed his mind about them (not surprisingly!) since crossing over into the Spirit World.

Some mediums were too gifted for their own good: Helen Duncan for instance. This Scottish medium was doing so well at passing on accurate information from the Spirit World that the British government considered her a security risk during the Second World War.

In January 1944, the Admiralty in London intervened to put a stop to her successful readings. What alarmed the naval bigwigs was the way Helen could calmly transmit messages to people bereaved by battles on land, sea, and in the air.

From the beginning of the war, she had conveyed the good news to bereaved relatives of men killed in action that their loved ones were healed in the Spirit World.

One sitting really infuriated the military chiefs: A sailor came through and informed relatives that his ship; the HMS Bahrnam had been sunk a few days before.

The Admiralty was mortified when it heard about this because the sinking of the ship had not yet been made public, and the dead sailor's mother had not been officially notified of his death.

It feared that if she could elicit information on an event of this kind that was a "classified secret", she might also be capable of picking up messages from people in the Spirit World sympathetic to Hitler and that such information might then find its way to German intelligence.

Shortly after this remarkable reading for the sailor's family, the police raided a room where Helen Duncan was holding another sèance. She was arrested, taken into custody and charged under the Witchcraft Act of 1735.

A total of 41 people who had been consoled by Helen's mediumship spoke up for her at the trial. They all pleaded for mercy and compassion, hoping that common sense would prevail. They testified that she was an excellent medium who had comforted hundreds of bereaved families by offering proof of survival. They described the sèances where Helen had acted as a channel for their loved ones and at which materialisations had occurred.

But the Judge and Jury paid no attention to them. Helen Duncan was found guilty of contravening the Witchcraft Act. Though a frail woman with six children, Helen was sentenced to nine months in jail and her family was evicted from their home.

Upon her release, she was forced to keep a low profile for the duration of the war as the Government continued to deem her gift a "security risk".

After the war, she suffered further persecution. In 1956, a private house in Nottingham where she was holding a sèance was raided while she was in deep trance. Helen was emotionally shattered and traumatised by this interruption. She died five weeks later.

Thank God, attitudes to mediums have changed for better in recent decades. The case of Helen Duncan serves as a reminder of how ignorance, misunderstanding, and blind, unreasoning prejudice have ruined the lives of many good people who used their psychic powers for the betterment of humanity:

All the more reason to treasure and respect the REAL mediums we have with us today and not allow this great gift to be defamed or misrepresented by chancers posing as psychics!

There were -and are- obvious differences between mental mediumship and physical mediumship. People have always felt more comfortable with the former than with the latter. It is the best-known mode of communication with the Spirit World.

It involves the use of clairaudience, in some cases clairvoyance, and occasionally the gifts known as automatic writing and automatic speech.

In my own case, I am privileged to be gifted with a multiplicity of psychic faculties: clairvoyance, clairaudience, and clairsentience, in addition to having the power to bring healing to people afflicted by illness of the body or mind.

I explain the meanings of these strange-sounding terms elsewhere in the book.

Physical mediumship is less common nowadays than it was in the early days of spiritualism. It is famous for the dramatic and possibly unnerving movement of objects by the medium during sèances.

Also less familiar in recent times, but very real, is the practise of materialisation: This involves the actual appearance of spirit people in the sèance room where they become visible to non-psychics who are present. The apparitions resemble deceased loved ones in every detail.

The rare process of direct voice mediumship provides some of the best evidence for survival, certainly from the point of view of anyone reluctant to accept the reality of an afterlife. This is where the spirit people speak directly to loved ones and others gathered around the medium.

While the majority of the mediums who worked in the early days of spiritualism were genuine, a few unscrupulous frauds motivated only by a desire to "get rich quick" also got in on the act.

These were easily exposed, but unfortunately they made life very difficult for the honest and gifted mediums who helped many people come to terms with the loss of loved ones.

The shameful activities of fraudsters had the effect of encouraging the sceptics and atheists and generating cynicism among those who had been prepared to keep an open mind about the paranormal.

As a result of this negative behaviour, the spiritualist movement lost a lot of ground in America, Britain, and elsewhere.

But it experienced a welcome revival towards the end of the 20th century with the ushering in of a new age of enlightened thinking and what has come to be referred to as cosmic consciousness.

In my own practise, I operate independently of the various religions and belief systems-adhering strictly to the truth, the simple, unvarnished truth of communication with the Spirit World.

When I do readings, I am attentive to the voices of departed loved ones, and the messages that come through. I never try to convert people to any religious belief, or attempt to persuade them that any one religion is better than another.

A person can be a follower of any set of beliefs on earth and yet believe or accept the simple fact that people on the other side can communicate with people here on earth.

The only "truth" I bring to people at readings is the good news that their "deceased" loved ones are alive and well in a safe place- in a world that is hidden from view for the moment but that is very real; a place that is beautiful beyond their wildest dreams.

And I don't even need to convert anyone to that belief: It becomes a self-evident reality once the messages start coming through!

CHAPTER 21

To All Sceptics:
Food for Thought ...

ADIEHARD sceptic will probably never accept the reality of life after death. But he would do well to consider some scientifically accepted facts that lend weight to what every medium knows: that energy is never destroyed, regardless of outward appearances and what we think we see happening.

A simple example will illustrate the truth of this: if we take a cardboard box and tear it up into four or five smaller sections, the parts still exist.

If you then burn the lot, you still have not destroyed the energies that came together to form the box. There have been physical alterations to the matter that composed the box caused by combustion, a chemical process. We look at the remnants of the cardboard box and think: that's the end of that. Now it's just a handful of ashes.

But we have not destroyed the energies, just scattered them. Many of the individual atoms that made up the box have been dispersed into the atmosphere around us. We can't see them, but they are there. Other atoms comprise the small heap of ashes that we think of as the annihilated box.

We see the ashes, but we can't perceive the equally real and solid part of the box that has been transformed by the act of burning. The reason we can't see it is because the energies are more thinly dispersed than when they formed PART of what we knew as the cardboard box.

These energies are now invisible to the naked eye, but as real as the visible handful of ashes.

To follow this analogy through, we can liken the ashes to a physical body that has been vacated at death. And the atoms of the box that continue to exist undamaged and indestructible as the spirit that survives death.

The sceptic asks: how can other levels of existence be out there if most people (non-clairvoyants) can't see them? Why should we believe in the existence of the Spirit World if astronomers can't see it through a telescope or if samples of matter from it can't be studied under a laboratory microscope?

Again, I refer our sceptical friend to the teachings and laws of orthodox science. We don't see the air we breathe, but it's there. We don't see the many energies that exist in the atmosphere around us, such as electricity, x rays, laser beams, microwaves, radio transmissions, to name but a few; but none of us will dispute their objective reality.

In the same way, the average person cannot see or hear spirit beings because we are dealing here with different energy manifestations that are invisible and inaudible to the majority of human beings.

The sights and sounds are on a higher vibratory level. Just as animals can hear sounds a human cannot, so also a clairaudient person can tune into higher sonic frequencies. And a clairvoyant can see what to a non-psychic person would be invisible.

But to deny the existence of an energy-manifestation because one cannot directly perceive it is totally unreasonable.

One could, if adopting that attitude; reject the existence of all those invisible energies that abound in the universe, just as scientists for long ridiculed the idea that clairvoyants could perceive a multi-coloured aura that surrounds every living being.

Nonsense, they laughed, and described the aura as a figment of wild imaginings and superstition.

But they stopped laughing at the clairvoyants when a camera was developed a few years ago that could actually photograph the aura. Now we can have our auras photographed any day of the week and look at those swirling vortices of energy that can serve as an index to our health and spiritual well being.

The psychics had been right all along about the aura, just as we told the truth-and still do-about that world beyond the grave that awaits all of us.

SCIENTISTS WHO SAID YES TO AN AFTERLIFE

Among the scientists convinced of the evidence for an afterlife were Alfred Wallace, Arthur Findlay, Professor Albert Einstein, Sir Arthur Conan Doyle, Professor William James Marconi, Lord Balfour, Sir Oliver Lodge, Lord Raleigh, and J.J. Thompson. Thompson revolutionised science by discovering the electron.

These renowned scientists and intellectuals worked in different fields of study and research but had one common interest that motivated and inspired them: They were pioneers of psychic research who were dedicated to scientifically investigating the evidence for life after death. Wishful thinking played no part in their investigations. Nor did the teachings or beliefs of any one religion. They set out with open minds and a healthy dose of scepticism, approaching the subject occasionally with unease or hesitation ... but they were always willing to accept their findings, however challenging, unorthodox, scientifically embarrassing or controversial these might prove to be.

Alternative explanations were examined in every case of miraculous or paranormal activity brought to their attention. Fraud of any kind was ruthlessly exposed and eliminated from the equation. But after long and exhaustive study, research, and experimentation, they concluded that the afterlife was a reality. The weight of evidence was overwhelming. The psychics and the genuine mediums-the gifted ones-were found to be telling the truth.

A classic investigator of the afterlife was Emmanuel Swedenborg, a leading Swedish scientist of the early 18th century.

He wrote 150 books dealing with every branch of science. He was centuries ahead of his time, having invented the glider, among other innovative or futuristic contrivances. He was a respected member of parliament who held top positions in the Swedish government.

But it is for his extraordinary lifelong devotion to investigating the Spirit World and all aspects of the paranormal that he is best remembered. Swedenborg had strong clairvoyant powers that he used to gain knowledge of other dimensions.

For over twenty years, he communicated with spirit people, holding regular two-way conversations with the "dead".

In one of his books dealing with his own experience of the paranormal, he wrote: " ... After the spirit has been separated from the body, he is still alive, a person, the way he was before.

"To assure me of this, I have been allowed to talk with practically everyone I have ever known during this physical life - with some for hours, with some for weeks or months, with some for years - all for the overriding purpose that I might be assured of this fact: that life persists after death ... "

Swedenborg wrote of his numerous Out of Body Experiences, some of which offered a graphic description of the spirit world.

Perhaps one of the greatest minds of the 20th century was Thomas Edison, the famed American inventor of the phonograph and the electric light bulb. He was also a spiritualist who accepted the existence of other dimensions.

He believed that one day a mechanical device capable of contacting the Spirit World would be invented. His own researches convinced him that such a phone-like contrivance was feasible.

After Edison's death, John Logie Baird, who pioneered television and invented the infrared camera, succeeded in making contact with the great inventor at a sèance!

Dr Glen Hamilton, a noted Canadian physician, carried out experiments under strict laboratory conditions. Photographs were taken of spirits materialising in a room in which a host of eminent observers had gathered to attest to the validity of the phenomenon.

Fourteen electronically operated flash cameras that snapped simultaneously photographed the apparitions. Sceptics and believers alike were stunned by the resulting pictures, which again offered evidence of survival.

Observers, who included medical doctors and electrical engineers, actually saw the spirits appearing and also confirmed that no trickery was involved. Details of Dr. Hamilton's research and the precious, authentic spirit photographs are displayed publicly at the University of Manitoba in Canada.

Each year, thousands of visitors call to examine these pictures that provide a window into another world. I have similar snaps taken in my home that show spirit forms. For people who are not clairvoyant, they offer proof that a world unseen by most humans really does exist all around them.

Dr Elisabeth Kubler-Ross, who has had a positive influence worldwide on how we view, and treat, the dying, came to believe in an afterlife as a result of her close contact with thousands of patients. In a 1997 book, she described her conversion to a belief in an afterlife. Early in her work, Dr. Ross had disregarded all the teachings about life after death. But gradually she arrived at the conclusion that the visions and perceptions of dying people were not merely hallucinations or delusions caused by medication. She was touched, and then totally convinced, by their sincerity.

She came to accept what mediums had known for centuries: that people who are close to death may see their loved ones on the other side preparing to welcome them.

DIRECT VOICE ... THE SPIRIT SPEAKS!

Direct voice mediums, though very rare, have added considerably to the volume of evidence for survival of death.

As mentioned in a previous chapter, people present at a direct voice session can hear the actual voices of their loved ones, or of other human beings who have died. Ectoplasm produced by the medium is used to create a temporary voice box to enable the spirits to be heard.

Englishman John Sloan was a famous direct voice medium. It was he who converted Arthur Findlay, an agnostic stockbroker, to a belief in an afterlife. Mr. Findlay went on to become a renowned researcher into all aspects of the paranormal.

He decided Sloan was genuine after hearing his deceased father's voice at a sitting. His father passed on messages containing information that could not possibly have originated from any other source.

Mr. Findlay was so impressed by what he heard and experienced that he embarked on a wide-ranging, internationally acclaimed study of psychic phenomena.

His book On the Edge of the Etheric, published in 1930, offered a brilliant scientific and totally objective analysis of the work of mediums and others who establish contact with the Spirit World. The Arthur Findlay College, at which I have given tutorials, is named in honour of this groundbreaking author and researcher.

Leslie Flint, another direct voice medium, submitted to countless laboratory tests to prove that his gift was genuine.

He had his mouth taped during some sittings, and in others full of water, at the same time having his hands and feet bound tightly, to demonstrate that he could not be producing any of the voices by ventriloquism or trickery of any kind.

Despite these and countless other ingenious restrictions thought up by sceptics and scientists anxious to disprove his gift, people in his presence when he went into trance continued to hear the voices from the Spirit World.

In some of the experiments in which his lips were sealed and his hands and feet bound, the voices actually spoke more clearly and loudly as if to prove a point!

Thousands of these clear, evidential messages were recorded during his lifetime: Many of the spirit people who came through spoke in languages or dialects unknown to Mr. Flint, and some of the languages were unfamiliar to the numerous linguistic experts who listened to and analysed the tapes.

These were found to have been ancient tongues that had long since become extinct.

Leslie Flint never ceased to be amazed at the lengths that sceptics and detractors were prepared to go in their efforts to find fault with, or denigrate, his mediumship. First, they alleged that perhaps the voices were unreal, being the result of hypnosis on his part and delusions or auditory hallucinations on the part of sitters or audiences.

This alternative explanation was easily disproved by the fact that the voices were captured on tape.

The allegation that he might have been a ventriloquist was blown away when he agreed to have a throat microphone attached to his throat to register even the slightest sound he could make through his larynx. The device was capable of greatly amplifying any sound he tried to make during the sitting.

During this experiment, observers that included technical experts and scientists watched him carefully through an infrared telescope. Throughout the sitting, the voices came as loud and clear as ever. Yet no movement or sound was detected in his throat.

William R. Bennett, Professor of Electrical Engineering at Colombia University in New York City, investigated Leslie Flint with a view to ascertaining if any explanation other than the spiritual one might emerge from experiments.

The sceptics awaited the outcome of his tests with great interest. They believed that this respected engineer who had a reputation to live up to would surely put Leslie Flint out of commission.

But Professor Bennett confounded the sceptics with his findings. He wrote: "My experience with Mr Flint is first hand; I have heard the independent voices. Furthermore, modern investigation techniques not available in earlier tests corroborate previous conclusions by indicating that the voices are not his. "The suggestion of accomplices became untenable for me during his visit to New York in September 1970, when, in an impromptu séance in my apartment, the same voices not only appeared but took part in conversations with the guests".

So there it was: Instead of disproving spirit communication, every test carried out on Leslie Flint served rather to strengthen the case for survival of bodily death, a truth known to us mediums for centuries but rejected by sceptics for whom no amount of evidence will suffice to change their minds.

No matter ... They will learn the truth firsthand when they cross over into the Spirit World. It will be a pleasant surprise for them to discover that life on the earth plane is just a phase in their eternal cosmic destiny.

Having fought so hard to maintain their view that death is the end, they will, hopefully rejoice in being proved wrong once they perceive the glory that God has prepared for all of us on the Other Side. Anyone can make a mistake!

VOICES ON TAPE

Further evidence to confound the sceptics has been gleaned from Electronic Voice Phenomena or EVP. For more than half a century, psychic researchers and experimenters across the globe have been recording voices on tape claiming to be those of spirit people.

The voices cannot be heard when the machine is running, but when the tape is played back, the voices are heard. Many of the messages come from deceased relatives or friends of the experimenters. They want them to know of their continued existence beyond the grave.

I can personally attest to the validity of this phenomenon: Since I began taping readings for clients, I have, from time to time heard voices other than my own or the sitter on the tapes.

The spirits can sometimes impress themselves on the tape as part of an attempt on their part to communicate the good news of their survival.

People take away the tapes to listen to the reading again and are amazed, occasionally, to hear "third parties" interrupting.

It is good to know that there are now thousands of open-minded investigators worldwide researching this form of spirit communication. Strict scientific procedures are applied in the experiments and the voices are recorded in laboratories and/or soundproof rooms.

Cynical or atheistic people are among those involved in the experiments and some of them get the shock of their lives-or a pleasant surprise, depending on how they take it- when the voice of a loved one comes through on tape!

In 1971, a book called Breakthrough caused ripples in the international scientific community and proved an important boost to psychic research. The author was Dr. Constantine Raudive, a Swede, who had recorded the grand total of 72,000 mysterious voices on tape.

He recounts the painstaking work in his book, which confounded the sceptics with its carefully documented cases suggestive of spirit communication by means of technology. Raudive's groundbreaking research provoked a worldwide interest in Electronic Voice Phenomena.

The first EVP experiments were undertaken in the 1920s. Thomas Edison speculated that there might be an unknown frequency somewhere between the long and short waves that might enable contact to be established with other dimensions.

The first spirit voices were recorded in 1938. They turned up on phonograph records. By the early 1950s, the voices started manifesting on tape recorders. Though not expressing public approval of EVP experiments, even the Vatican, to its credit, took a behind the scenes interest in the subject.

In 1952, two Italian priests were recording Gregorian chant in an abbey when they discovered voices other than the singers on the tape. Father Gemelli heard his deceased father speak.

The priests, concerned that spirit communication might contravene Catholic teaching, called to Pope Pius XII in Rome to explain what had happened. The Pope asked them not to worry about it, since a tape recorder was an objective instrument and merely recorded whatever sounds or voices it picked up.

Pope Paul VI took a keen interest in EVP after hearing of experiments conducted by a friend of his, the Swedish film producer Friedrich Jorgensen, a Knight Commander of the Order of St Gregory.

The Vatican allowed its own priests to research EVP. A Swiss theologian, Father Leo Schmidt, recorded more than ten thousand discarnate voices. Details of his work are recounted in a book entitled When the Dead Speak, published in 1976.

Since the 1970s, the Vatican has adopted a tolerant view of parapsychology, even allowing courses on the subject for priests. In 1997, a leading theologian in the Vatican, Father Gino Concetti was asked about his opinion of EVP in an interview.

He said: "According to the modern catechism, God allows our dear departed persons who live in an ultra-terrestrial dimension, to send messages to guide us in certain difficult moments of our lives.

The Church has decided not to forbid any more the dialogue with the deceased on condition that these contacts are carried out with a serious religious and scientific purpose".

Internet websites on EVP abound, and there are numerous books on the subject. Anyone who honestly believes that death is the end should listen to some of these tape recordings.

They confirm what I, as a medium, have known since childhood: that our loved ones can speak to us and let us know that life goes on ... whether through a medium such as myself, in dreams, or by means of technology.

They will always find a way to get through to us.

CHAPTER 22

Betrayals in Love and Friendship

A T MANY readings I have listened to sad, maze-like, and sometimes devastating tales of betrayal, whether in extramarital affairs or friendships. We all suffer betrayals in life.

At one time or another, we experience the full impact of deception, broken promises, devious behaviour, and crushing disillusionment, inflicted by fellow human beings who believe they can get away with this malevolent, nasty, and spiteful abuse of TRUST.

And of course we are equally capable of betraying others. Betrayal is one of the nastiest behavioural traits of the human species.

I remember in my childhood listening to my mother tell stories about how some locals in Graiguenamanagh, as indeed in the rest of Ireland, betrayed their neighbours or fellow countrymen and women throughout history.

In every situation where you had brave people who would sacrifice anything, including their very lives, for what they believed in, you also had the betrayers.

In Cromwell's time, monks were betrayed for gold and silver by people they knew and trusted. They went to their deaths because of human greed and treachery.

When the Black and Tans came to Ireland in 1920, they made frequent raids on my mother's family home in Harristown, Graiguenamanagh. My grandparents' home was always the first to be raided when the troops drove into town.

The dreaded Crossley Tenders pulled up in the street and the Tans spilled out of these ancient lorries to take up positions in front of suspect homes. They always came without warning ... but somebody somewhere knew they were coming ... the betrayer who had tipped them off or sold them the vital information.

My mother had a vivid recollection of the soldiers rampaging through the house: Locals who saw the chance of earning a few bob on the side occasionally informed on people suspected of being rebels.

One woman is supposed to have worked out an elaborate system of signals by which she pinpointed for the Tans the exact locations of rebel households: She spilled milk outside the entrances to their homes.

This betrayal then led the vengeful Tans to the doors of patriotic people who "got the works". All they had to do was follow the trail of milk!

Betrayal in times of political crisis or national emergency is bad enough ... but at least the betrayers have the excuse of being tempted by money, or they may be compelled to inform on people they know. Torture has always been a great persuader.

Betrayals in relationships can inflict even more pain because they tend to involve "nearest and dearest": In the case of marriage, someone to whom we have pledged lifelong love and fidelity.

I have listened to many tales of woe on this subject ... to a never-ending story of deceit, perfidy, and duplicity. On reflection, perhaps the wording of the marriage vow should be amended to read: "Till death OR BETRAYAL do us part ... "

Men have come to tell me of affairs ... Some ask me if their lovers will leave their husbands for them.

They are desperately anxious to know how far their secret lovers will go along the road of fulfilling their need for their dishonest, clandestine relationship ... but don't seem remotely concerned about their own wives, and the dishonesty that such cheating entails.

They get upset or seem uncomfortable if I suggest that they tell their wives that they wish to end the relationship.

They don't want to know. The degree of utter selfishness and ruthless egotism never ceases to amaze me. Another case comes to mind: A woman with no children was expecting her first child after 14 years of marriage.

Her husband meanwhile was having an affair with his best friend's wife, but didn't care about his own wife, or how she might be hurt by his infidelity.

That affair was obviously heading into perilous waters. Two or more families could have been wrecked and traumatised by the inevitable, eventual "outing" of all the conniving, double-crossing, and treachery.

I have met women too who raised their children, while at the same time managing to have one or more affairs going on the side. They appear to give little or no thought to the unfairness of this deceitful arrangement.

I ask people why they need to have affairs if they are happily married. They say, in effect, that they like it that way! I find this offensive and shocking.

Some men, hard to believe, can carry on two or three affairs without their wives suspecting a thing. Though it might be tempting to ridicule a woman who is so completely conned, many women are completely trusting, and steadfastly loyal to their husbands or partners.

They simply have never even considered the possibility that their darlings would be cheating on them! And their partners cynically use and abuse their naivety and trusting natures, exploiting their very innocence to conceal from them the cruel truth of infidelity. I've met people also who will not leave husbands or wives despite having regular affairs. They remain married to the same partner for life, while cheating to their hearts' content.

There are others who live in a false but never quenching hope that their lovers will leave marriages for them. They may go all the way into old age wishing and longing for this illusive outcome.

Anyone hurt by infidelity can find it difficult to discuss his/her ordeal with another person. They feel isolated, angry, embarrassed, and overwhelmed by disbelief that they have been fooled and betrayed in such a calculated way by someone they loved or trusted.

The exposure of a partner's deadly secret comes like a hammer blow, a cruel, emotionally shattering kick in the teeth.

The betrayed partner then has to decide whether to forgive, if the other person appears truly sorry, or to break off the relationship. All sorts of factors have a bearing on that decision, such as the strength or weakness of the betrayed partner's love, his/her religious belief, financial circumstances, emotional dependency, and so on.

I advise people affected by betrayal to seek counselling. Every case is different. But I can assure anyone out there who is currently abusing a relationship, marriage, or friendship with secret betrayal that you will be found out-eventually.

Whether it takes weeks, months, years, or even decades, the secret will ALWAYS be revealed. It is a natural law of the universe that secrets can only be withheld and covered up for so long.

The longer a secret is hidden, the worse its negative impact will be when the day of reckoning arrives. Then, the victim of betrayal or deceit or trickery will see your past actions and words in the cold light of truth.

If you are being unfaithful to a wife, husband, or partner, I advise you to own up immediately. Cut your losses and admit the truth, however painful that may be.

If you find this course of action difficult or impossible to contemplate, think of the far greater and more painful consequence – for you and your partner – of having him or her discover your betrayal by accident – or through malicious gossip of neighbours or busybodies.

If you are leading a trusting, loving partner up the garden path, put down this book now and pick up the phone: Admit your wrongdoing and humbly beg forgiveness. If you are lucky, you may receive pardon and a second chance – whether you deserve it or not.

Words cannot describe the hurt sustained as a consequence of a long-drawn out act of betrayal or infidelity. One to one or group counselling is available to victims of this rat-like behaviour. But prevention is always better than cure.

You can ease the pain of betrayal by coming clean with that other human being who has loved and trusted you.

Remember that a callously betrayed person may commit suicide, or sink into a deep depression that may last a lifetime. And the betrayer will then have this guilty stain on his conscience, also perhaps for life.

Friendships are equally prone to betrayal. In fact, friends can deal us the biggest letdowns. The longer the friendship, the greater will be the sense of hurt and shock when the axe of betrayal falls. As in a relationship, trust has been shattered.

The true nature of the friendship can dictate the form the betrayal will take. It may be that your supposed "friend" has never been what he seemed. He may have been simply using or manipulating you to suit his own purposes. The act of betrayal could well represent the culmination of a long drawn out false friendship that was always destined to end in tears.

Such friendships can endure for months, even years, before the impostor is unmasked by a single treacherous deed: It may involve a breach of confidence, however minor, that brings it home to you that this person cannot be trusted, and that you were foolish to ever have trusted him/her with your innermost thoughts, feelings, secrets, or desires. To lead somebody up the garden-path, or along the road of false friendship, abusing their good will and trust, is an act of calculated cruelty. If you consciously deceive a fellow human in this way, you are accumulating a lot of negative moral baggage for yourself.

As in every other life situation, you will have to reap the mistrust, the hurt, and crushing disillusionment that you have sown. If you sow seeds of deception, betrayal, and false friendship, you will someday reap a harvest of torment, mental anguish, and treachery for yourself.

What goes around comes around: He who betrays today will be a victim of betrayal. The cosmic law of cause and effect is immutable.

Then again, forgiveness may be in order if your friend was genuine and has simply acted selfishly on a once off basis to let you down. Falling out with somebody over a minor hiccup in a friendship is unjustified.

None of us are perfect, and there is no point in over-reacting to a silly remark or perceived disloyalty by building it up into a melodramatic scenario that is out of all proportion to the real issue.

A friend who has lapsed, or erred in a perfectly human way is not in the same category as the malicious "user" and manipulator, the kind of guy-or woman-of whom one could truly say: With a "friend" like that, who needs enemies?"

One final point about betrayal: If you have been betrayed by a friend or lover, you may feel a justifiable sense of rage, an overpowering desire to get even and wreak a terrible vengeance.

I advise you to put aside all such thoughts of revenge. Remember what Jesus said about "loving your enemies?" The great teachers of other religions offered similar advice. You have nothing to gain by descending to the level of the betrayer.

While the thought of actually loving those who have hurt you may be a little hard for most people to stomach, you should definitely think twice before drawing up plans to "do down" a person who has wronged you.

Rest easy in the knowledge that he or she will have to answer for the betrayal, both in this life – by being on the receiving end of the same type of treatment – and most definitely in the Spirit World where they will be called on to account for their unfair dealings with you.

If you can, try to gain from the experience of betrayal: See it as a test, yet another of those hurdles that you need to surmount in your evolution as a spirit in a human body.

Instead of being consumed by bitterness and hatred, you can look upon this treacherous " bolt from the blue" as a challenge, an opportunity for spiritual growth that will make you a better person.

Look at it this way: It will help you to understand, and empathise with, other victims of betrayal. Without such direct experience of the emotional responses it provokes and draws forth, we would not be as well placed to help, advise, or comfort our fellow human beings who need our support when they are hit by that same poisoned arrow.

Like every knock and setback we suffer on the earth plane, this one must be seen in the context of life's overall purpose and design: We are here to learn and mature as spiritual beings. So we must take the good with the bad.

So please allow God's justice to take its course. By giving in to feelings of hatred, you are just taking on the baggage and negativity of the person who has betrayed you. There is no need for you to get even. Let your anger subside. A good way of coping with the anger of betrayal is to have a punching bag in your house or garden.

If you feel the need to give vent to your anger, just belt away at the punch bag for a while. Get all that rage out of your system. You'll feel great after it.

When you've exhausted yourself; sit back, relax, and think of that old Jewish proverb: "Forgive your enemies … but remember their names!"

If the hurt inflicted goes much deeper and you feel you cannot cope, then seek help or counselling. Do not hesitate to reach out. It's your life. You are entitled to happiness and peace of mind. So be content. Learn to trust again, and know that there are plenty of decent folk out there who don't betray their friends or partners.

CHAPTER 23

The Crime that Dare Not Speak its Name

The painful issue of sexual abuse, both in institutions and within families, has dominated media headlines in recent years. Though it is only in the past decade or so that quite a few horrific cases have come to light, the problem has been around since the dawn of civilisation.

Though I deal with betrayal in a separate chapter, mainly concerning love and friendship, the greatest betrayal of all is that perpetrated by a person who sexually abuses a family member or a child or teenager who has been entrusted to his/her care, whether in a home or in a religious or state run institution.

To inflict the horrors of sexual abuse on a defenceless victim in any situation is the ultimate act of nauseating evil ... For years in Ireland, for far too long, it was the hidden crime ... the crime that dare not speak its name.

But then the truth began to emerge ... in slow, nightmarish instalments ... We heard first about one or two incidents where priests or Christian Brothers had abused boys in orphanages or even within the sacred walls of Catholic churches.

Gradually, more cases emerged, brought to light in a revolting but necessarily graphic series of TV programmes and newspaper exposes that lifted the lid on the widespread abuse that had been concealed or swept under the carpet.

The award-winning States of Fear programme featured interviews with former residents, male and female, of industrial schools around Ireland. They had been beaten, humiliated, and sexually abused by individuals the rest of society regarded at the time as "holy people" who could do no wrong.

The priest, brother, or nun, was someone you saluted and took your hat off to if they passed you in the street. The idea that religious folk could wreak such havoc on the lives of innocent children was unthinkable. But the truth came out, as it always does ... eventually. Now we have special redress boards, counselling services, and help-lines attempting to offer support and healing to the abuse victims. At readings, former nuns or male religious teachers have come through from the Spirit World to beg forgiveness of ex-pupils who they punished too severely at school. It is up to the ex-pupils whether to absolve them of their guilt and pardon their despicable past behaviour.

But while institutional abuse is at last being confronted in Irish society, the same problem when it occurs within families can still, even in our supposedly enlightened age, be a taboo subject.

I have had many people with me over the years who told of unspeakable crimes inflicted on them by fathers, grandfathers, uncles, or elder brothers. Women can be abusers too, of course, but the majority tend to be male.

The nature of the crime is such that victims may well feel ashamed to speak of their ordeal. Abuses can remain undetected, even by close friends and other family members, for many years until the victim is ready to blow the whistle on them.

As a medium, I see another and almost unbearably distressing side to this cowardly crime. Victims have broken down, recalling the hell they went through, and the feeling of total helplessness that held them back whenever they even considered exposing the cruel excuse for a human being who was tearing their lives apart.

The abusers were in complete control, believing the victims would never speak out, or that if they did, nobody would believe them anyway.

But in addition to hearing, and empathising with, the horror stories of sexual abuse victims, I have also been permitted to look beyond this earth plane and see what has become of abusers who passed over.

What a sorry plight these offenders find themselves in once they leave behind the planet upon which they wrought their sexual perversions. What a rude and terrible awakening awaits all abusers on the Other Side!

They are dealt with severely, being confined to the darker levels of the afterlife where there is much "wailing and gnashing of teeth" to cite the old expression. Not for them the joys of the Spirit World that await the vast majority of human beings.

They have to live with the awful consequences of their actions. They get to see-and partly experience – the pain and suffering they inflicted on their victims.

Any abuser here on earth who could clairvoyantly see what I have seen of their direful predicament "over there" would reform himself or herself very quickly indeed.

How long they remain in the twilight regions after death will depend to a large extent on their victims. Forgiveness may loosen their bonds and help to set them free from their self-imposed torment.

I witness the sad spectacle of abusers in the Spirit World beseeching the families of victims on earth to forgive them. At readings, I have listened to the wailing and pleading from these tormented souls, begging and crying out for pardon to victims sitting opposite me.

Forgiveness may or may not be forthcoming, depending on the severity of the abuse or the psychological make-up of the person who has suffered it.

In a typical case, half the family members might be willing to forgive a close relative who has abused one of them, but the rest of the family may be adamant that no mercy be shown to him. I have seen and felt the bitterness of people who say "Never!" when asked by an abuser on the Other Side to extend forgiveness.

I remember one harrowing case where an abuse victim flatly refused to forgive her father, who had perpetrated the crime against her. She literally stamped on the floor in anger, rejecting his pleas for mercy.

I could hear the father sobbing, pleading, beseeching ... all to no avail. It is up to this woman to seek therapy. Perhaps, in time, she may pardon her father.

The lack of forgiveness holds back the perpetrator of such crimes, who is confined to the lowest level of the Spirit World until the time is right to move on.

Though it is better to forgive, I can understand the reluctance of people to forgive or forget or pardon the trauma and unbearable suffering wrought by sexual abuse. The victims of abuse very often turn to drugs or violence themselves, or have their lives otherwise destroyed as a result of their ordeal.

They feel they cannot cope, or come to terms with the wrong that has been inflicted on them.

Yet I advocate forgiveness. By forgiving, you become a better person and will advance further along the path to spiritual enlightenment. It is difficult and painful, but a necessary part of the healing process.

PHYSICAL AND PSYCHOLOGICAL ABUSE IN THE HOME

It has been said that: "we hurt the ones we love". Perhaps, but there are degrees of hurt and there are limits to the amount of punishment that any of us should have to put up with.

Physical abuse in a marriage or relationship can take the forms of shaking, shoving, punching, bruising, kicking, or attempted strangulation, or hitting the person with any object that serves as a temporary weapon.

The use of this force is all about controlling the spouse or partner. Added to the physical abuse a victim may suffer humiliation and emotional trauma. This could take the form of sexual harassment, an excessively domineering attitude designed to control and oppress, or the continuous uttering of hurtful, degrading remarks to the victim.

These remarks or taunts may be of a sexual nature or directed against a perceived weak point in the victim's physical or psychological make-up. Name-calling is another tactic. The intention is always to humiliate and make the person feel small. Or the physical assaults may be accompanied by verbal or emotional abuse.

The abuser may also be more tactful and devious. Instead of resorting to physical force or verbal threats, he/she may resort to what is often referred to as "psychological battering" and cruel mind games designed to hurt the victim at a deeper level.

These sneak tactics could range from anything like hiding the car keys and stealing or hiding of clothes, or sadistically throwing out the dinner that has been prepared for him ... to secretly damaging or destroying objects in the house that have sentimental value to the abuse victim, or dropping persistent hints that the other person will lose custody of the children, killing their pet cat or dog, or telling malicious lies and innuendos to the victims' friends or relatives to "put them down".

All of this dysfunctional but extremely clever behaviour feeds the abuser's need for power over his victim and satisfies his control freak nature. The aim of this utterly sick and evil conduct towards a fellow human being is to keep the victim in a constant, debilitating state of fear.

Both the abuser and his victim conspire to keep the abuse hidden. A climate of denial grows and engulfs the couple. A victim will often not even tell a doctor or closest friend about the abuse.

Both, for their own reasons, want to prevent anyone else from learning the horrible truth, and yet the two of them are in need of urgent help. The victim is entitled to live in a non-threatening, abuse-free environment or relationship. She/he needs to seek support and counselling for this horrendous ordeal.

And the abuser must either face up to the true nature of his actions, whether physical or psychological, determine to stop hurting the other person AND seek professional help for his problem ... or otherwise be exposed publicly as an abuser by going to jail!

Only then can the cruel, nightmarish cycle of abuse be broken once and for all.

If you are a victim of emotional, physical, sexual, or psychological abuse in ANY relationship, you do not have to remain in that situation for one day longer.

Seek help today. Don't be afraid.

REMEMBER THE CHILDREN!

Apart from your own painful ordeal as an abuse victim, there is another reason why you should IMMEDIATELY move to break free of a domestic hell on earth.

If you are being abused, your children are suffering too, even if the effect of the abusive relationship is not visible or obvious to you. You have a serious, long-term responsibility to them, as well as to yourself.

By living in the same house where the abuse is taking place, the children will be open to the evil influence of domestic violence or bullying. Witnessing the abuse, be it physical or verbal, will subject them to the risk of psychological damage and emotional deprivation.

They can suffer ill health, difficulties at school, poor sleeping habits, aggression towards other children, low self-esteem, severe anxiety, or depression.

As a parent, you have a moral duty to safeguard your children from abusive situations, to educate them about the true nature of domestic violence and to discourage them from getting involved in violent, abusive relationships themselves.

They may also be at risk of being abused themselves by the same person who is hurting you, perhaps without your knowledge.

So think of these young ones too. By seeking help for yourself, and liberation from the torture chamber that the bully has created for you, you will also be saving your children from the future emotional scars that result from being reared in an abusive domestic environment.

WOMEN ABUSERS

It may come as a shock to some people to learn that there are plenty of female abusers out there as well.

The traditional view that men are always the perpetrators of sexual and physical abuse, and that women are the victims but never perpetrators, is one hundred percent false. It is also a dangerous notion because it helps aid the ongoing massive cover-up of abuse perpetrated by women. Despite the gentle, benign image that womanhood commands, it is a fact that the female of the species can often be as cruel, spiteful, vindictive, and ruthless as her male counterpart, sometimes far worse because she stands a greater chance of getting away with the abuse.

I know from my experience of many readings I have done over the years that women are perfectly capable of perpetrating acts of violence against other women, their own children, and against husbands and lovers. Unfortunately, they can be as devious as men too when it comes to the more subtle forms of domestic abuse.

Women are streets ahead of men when it comes to playing mind-games that can push a person to the brink of madness.

I have heard from people in the Spirit World about the atrocious misery and torment, wrought by molesting or physically abusive women, of mothers who sexually abused sons and daughters, and of "street angels" who hammered and thrashed their partners, beating them black and blue whenever the urge took them … while wearing sparkling haloes in their communities.

Some of these house tyrants were ladies who lined the front rows of churches, who were looked up to and revered as pillars of society. Butter wouldn't melt in their mouths, or so you would think if you saw them keeping up appearances and putting on a show for the outside world.

But once they get inside the front door, God help their victims, male or female, especially if the abuser happens to have had a bad day.

I have heard emotionally shattering stories from both sides of the Great Divide. In readings, victims who have since been healed in the Spirit World come through to either forgive their female tormenters or to express anger at the abuse.

And victims on the earth plane have directed their overwhelming, almost inexpressible rage against kith and kin on the other side who abused them in the past.

Incredibly, abusers grow into old age still denying the destructive effects of their behaviour. I know of some perpetrators who believed they would sail through the Gates of Heaven and plank themselves on the Golden Seats ... like they had done on earth, where they could hide their vicious behaviour from all but the victims.

They had, so they believed, absolved themselves of guilt by pretending to themselves, and others, that they had done nothing wrong. They were oblivious to the unfathomable evil of their crime.

Anyone, male or female, claiming to have been molested, beaten, or humiliated by a woman may find it difficult to be taken seriously or believed. All too often, the victims are accused of lying, exaggerating, or fabricating their experience.

In the case of a male partner who has suffered physical or emotional battering or sexual humiliation, his allegation may be dismissed as "unmanly" and "wimpish". He might be told to shut up for the sake of his public image and credibility:

"It wasn't abuse, honey, it was love!" is a notorious get-out clause often invoked by American female abusers, and a fair few Irish ladies are fond of trotting out the same excuse.

Men have been attacked with carving knives, thrown down stairs, and kicked senseless by domineering and abusive female partners. Children have seen their fathers being assaulted by their mothers, or their aunts beating up their uncles, and close female relatives have sexually abused children.

Male victims of cruel, ferocious, or conniving females come from all walks of life: high financiers, farmers, factory workers, tax collectors, trucks drivers ... men who help to run the country and men who sweep the streets ... or men who just stay at home to mind the children.

And they come from all age groups. Any man, woman, or child can be a victim of a female bully or abuser.

Men will go to any lengths to cover up the abuse. They'll say: Oh, I tripped and fell down the stairs ... or off a ladder ... or spilled boiling water and got roasted ... or sustained an injury while out jogging or on the sports field.

Any excuse will do ... as long as it protects a dark and shameful secret and lets his abusive wife or partner off the hook.

There have been cases- in Ireland and all over the world – where women who bullied and abused their husbands to the point of nervous breakdown or even death have not only gotten away with this crime – they succeeded in forcing the men to leave their homes ... despite the fact that it was they, the women, who were as guilty as sin.

Most men who break silence on their predicament generally do so when it is too late, after the abusive partner has finally triumphed in her reign of persecution and driven him to leave. Then the terrible stories of emotional, sexual, or psychological abuse begin to emerge.

The memories flood back and overwhelm them: They may suffer from depression, social disorientation, low self esteem, and a mental anguish that can last years if they fail to seek help.

Adults who either witnessed or experienced such abuse in childhood have come to me for readings, many of them in the hope of finding peace and healing, of somehow laying to rest the crime that ruined their lives.

When their abusers happen to communicate during the reading, they can release their pent-up anger.

Being a woman should not automatically confer immunity to blame for committing vicious crimes in the home or elsewhere.

While abuse of women by men must also be addressed, the tendency to demonise men and sanctify women is profoundly unhelpful and plays into the hands of female abusers.

Any man reading this who is a victim of spousal abuse should realise that he is not alone. Help is available. You are as entitled to that help and support as a woman who is victimised.

BLOWING THE WHISTLE ON ABUSERS

Another word on the issue of sexual abuse: As this is the most psychologically damaging form of abuse that occurs in the home, I would like to offer important advice and encouragement to anyone who has either been a victim of this crime, or who has knowledge or reliable information of such abuse.

Far too many people have, unknowingly, contributed to the concealing and even protection of sexual abuse by convincing themselves that exposing the crime would wreck families and create more problems than it would solve.

They say, in effect: Ah well, it's in the past now, what's the point in raking it all up again ... they imagine the "appalling vista" of families being ripped apart by the scandal if it goes to court and then hits the media headlines.

But while such fears and hesitations are understandable, they play directly into the hands of the abusers.

You may think that an abuse situation is "in the past", but you cannot be sure: A person who has sexually abused another human being NEEDS TREATMENT, for his or her own sake and for the sake of every other potential victim that they will come into contact with throughout life.

There are brothers who abuse sisters. By remaining silent, to protect the family's image, their victims may inadvertently permit further abuse by those same people in the future.

What happens when these young offenders have families of their own? If they abused before, they can, and most likely WILL repeat the abuse when a suitable opportunity presents itself ... and this, quite likely, will be in another home setting... with their own children being the ones at high risk.

If the offenders had been confronted and given proper treatment earlier on, they might not have continued to destroy lives.

So please ... no matter when the abuse occurred, or no matter how much embarrassment you believe may be caused by blowing the whistle on abuse, do not hesitate to expose this evil.

You owe it to yourself and to your fellow human beings to cry "Halt" to this devilish crime if you are in a position to make a difference.

By exposing past abuses that have been swept under the carpet, you will be achieving a double victory over this horrendous betrayal of the weak by the strong: You will help to deter potential abuse by setting an example of justice being done ... and you will prevent the individual abuser from ever again gaining access to the vulnerable people he or she has targeted in the past.

You will also be helping to ensure that the abuser, who must some day cross over into the Greater Life, will have paid part of his spiritual debt here on earth.

There are help-lines and contact numbers at the front of this book: If you feel you can assist in bringing abusers to justice, or in helping a victim (yourself or anyone else), phone the relevant agency or organisation today. You will be a better person for it!

CHAPTER 24

Bullying in the School and Workplace

W RITING OF my childhood days, I recalled the severity of the Convent regime, and the nuns who had a fondness for the pointer and leather strap.

Today, attending school can also be a nightmare for children. But for a different reason: Fear of the bullies that make their presence felt in classrooms and schoolyards nationwide. Bullying is an evil that plights the lives of school goers and their families.

Over the years, many parents have told me of the unspeakable ordeals to which their children have been subjected. I tend to refer such people to doctors or counsellors, as they may need urgent help and support of a non-spiritual nature.

The children are humiliated and terrorised by fellow pupils. As a result, they suffer in a variety of ways: ranging from frustration, social isolation and loss of self-esteem to drastic personality changes, illness, depression and, the ultimate tragedy: suicide.

They lose motivation, are fearful and anxious about going to school, or may suffer stomach or bowel disorders, panic attacks, depression, unnatural mood swings, or nervous breakdowns. Some pupils resort to substance abuse and end up as drug addicts.

I would advise any parents who are aware of such situations to make vigorous complaints to the school authorities, and, if possible, to seek counselling for the victims of bullying.

By the same token, of course, parents must ensure that none of their children become bullies themselves. Either way, parents have a moral duty to intervene to nip the problem in the bud if possible.

Bullies need help and counselling as well as their victims. If their parents fail to reprimand their behaviour, they are sending out the wrong signal: that it's okay to bully other children.

The great scandal is that quite a few people, whether in a school itself, or in the wider community, may know that bullying is going on, and who the victims are, and choose to remain silent about it. So the bullying continues until the victim reaches breaking point and just can't take any more punishment.

Whether the bullies taunt their victims, or physically hurt or injure them, the children on the receiving end of this treatment are liable to be emotionally shattered.

I have my own view on this: I believe that a separate body unconnected with school managements or individual teachers should be set up to stamp out bullying in schools.

Such a body should, I believe, be completely independent of the educational establishment. Officials appointed by it could visit schools to investigate complaints of bullying and interview all relevant personnel: The victims, the perpetrators, other pupils, the teachers, and the parents of both victims and the bullies.

The reason I favour an independent body or agency is that this would get around the obvious problem that arises from school authorities attempting to cover up instances of bullying. No school wants to have its reputation impugned, and the temptation must be there to deny and prevaricate. But an outside agency would cut through the smoke screens and get to the heart of the matter. I encourage any readers who agree with me to lobby or campaign for this more effective antidote to school bullying.

In the meantime, I would like to see awareness programmes in all primary and secondary schools aimed at tackling this dreadful and widespread abuse of children in the classrooms. Teachers need to be alert to the problem, and encourage classes to freely discuss bullying. It could form the theme of art projects and compositions.

Every child and teenager is entitled to an education. Having experienced a different form of bullying ... at the hands of teachers, I place a great value on what ought to be every person's birthright. Instead of being taught at school, some of us were beaten and made to feel inferior.

Instead of learning how to spell or to write, we learned the true meaning of fear. We learned how it feels to live in mortal dread of another human being. Learning can be fun. For us it was an ordeal, a penance to be endured.

Education should be the opposite of that: a life enhancing and positive experience. I hope and pray that this and future generations of Irish school children will be able to learn and grow in understanding of the world around them in a decent, responsible, and non-threatening environment.

BULLYING IN THE WORKPLACE

How nice and reassuring it would be if young adults could leave behind the nightmare of bullying once they leave school. But that is not the reality of this cruel, inhuman, and cowardly abuse of one's fellow human beings.

As in the school situation, bullying in the workplace can take many forms; but physical assault is less common than actions, remarks, or gestures that are intended to psychologically hurt, intimidate, degrade, humiliate or isolate the victim.

Workplace bullying often involves a discernable pattern of cruel victimisation of a person, or group of people, that the bully dislikes or of whom he/she is jealous.

Bullying can be overt and obvious, but also devious and subtle, hidden from all but the victims. Exhaustive research in Ireland and the rest of Europe, and in the USA, points to the following tactics employed by bullies to gain power over people in the workplace:

- The deliberate spreading of false, malicious rumours, and subtle innuendo about people;
- Seeking to exclude or socially isolate their victims;

- Aggressive or subtle intimidation by verbal or physical abuse;
- Constant threats and hurtful "bad taste" jokes to subdue a victim;
- Attempting to undermine the other person's work performance;
- Constantly changing work guidelines or areas of responsibility without just cause;
- Setting impossible deadlines to "trip up" the person;
- Withholding information from the victim or deliberately giving him/her misleading or false information;
- Persistent unfair criticism;
- Maliciously interfering with, or sabotaging, applications for promotion or training;
- Intrusions into a victim's privacy;
- Making the person feel useless or inadequate by undermining his or her self-confidence and making unwarranted comments about the standard of work.

As with school bullying, the workplace version has many short and long term effects; such as intense feelings of anger, shock, frustration, vulnerability, insomnia, headaches and stomach pains, panic attacks, anxiety, stress in the home and workplace, poor concentration, a collapse in morale and a consequent lowering of work performance.

If you are a victim of bullying, you can, if you feel up it, confront the bully and tell him/her that this behaviour is unacceptable. Warn them to either stop, or face a disciplinary hearing. Of course, that is easier said than done. It takes courage. Fear of the bully may be so ingrained and powerful that even the thought of facing him/her makes you cringe.

You might be advised to have somebody with you to witness your approach to the bully, to prevent any misrepresentation of what you have said to him/her, and to bear witness to the bully's response.

You could, alternatively, report the bully to either a supervisor or to your union, if you happen to be a member of one.

It is wise to keep a record or diary of all events and incidents that relate to the bullying. This should ideally include dates, times, and an accurate account of the bullying behaviour.

If you have received threatening letters, notes, faxes, or emails from the bully, be sure to hold on to all of these.

Though it will be tempting to hit back at the bully by striking him/her, or lashing out verbally in front of others, AVOID such retaliation.

It may not be understood as a legitimate response, or as a justifiable expression of anger on your part.

It may instead play into the hands of the bully, who can then allege that you are always "like that", and thus deserving of his/her bullying.

Stay within the law – keep a cool head – and you can beat the bully.

Employers have a moral and LEGAL obligation to protect workers from bullying. In theory, they are supposed to act decisively to eradicate this evil from the workplace. In practise, this obligation is often overlooked.

Worse still, the employer may be a personal friend of the bully or even be implicated in the bullying.

Employers should ENCOURAGE all staff and employees to report bullying. They ought to act speedily on any complaint received concerning such behaviour in the workplace, and offer full support to any victims of bullying.

If your employer fails to address the bullying issue and you are forced to quit your job because of intimidation, harassment, and stress, you can bring a case for unfair dismissal to the Employment Appeals Tribunal.

Remember, it's YOUR LIFE. Nobody has the right to take away your dignity as a human being. The bully, though he/she appears powerful and all conquering, is really a despicable grubby little coward.

Bullies only have the "power" that you allow them to have over you. They thrive on fear and secrecy ... by "keeping the thumb" on you.

If you are a victim of bullying, calmly assess the situation and follow the procedures outlined above.

With patience, and belief in yourself, you can break the stranglehold of fear and intimidation. You will regain your pride and self-worth.

Then it will be the bully's turn to run for cover!

CHAPTER 25

Accepting Differences

G AYS AND Lesbians call for readings. Many of them suffer terribly in their private and public lives. Some are driven to suicide by feelings of fear and shame associated with their dispositions.

They can feel like criminals, which they are not. Self-loathing is one of the consequences of heterosexual attitudes towards them. This in turn often leads to the emotional anguish and desolation of deep depression. They need to be aware at all times that their way of life is not an illness or an abnormality – just another mode of self-expression.

I have listened to many stories of heartache, prejudice, and misunderstanding concerning Gay and Lesbian people.

A typical traditional attitude is the parents' expectation of weddings in the family and a desire on their part to have their children become paragons of perfection, success, and "normality". They want the children to be a source of pride and joy, and not in any way "different".

It would probably be safe to say that few parents would actually WANT a child to be Gay. That sobering fact says a lot about the prevailing view of this misunderstood and still persecuted minority.

This attitude is all wrong. It must be borne in mind that many Gays are spirits who occupy the bodies of the opposite sex.

A man who finds himself attracted to other men may actually be a female spirit in a male body, and a Lesbian may be a male "trapped" in the body of a woman.

In each case, the spirit has incarnated on earth to meet certain challenges and learn certain lessons vital to his or her spiritual evolution. But the heterosexual community is being challenged too by the incarnation of their Gay fellow human beings.

The challenge is to avoid all forms of prejudice in our dealings with them, and to treat Gays and Lesbians at all times as equals.

I would urge their families, relatives, co-workers and indeed the rest of society to accept them in a non-judgemental way as equals and people entitled to justice, dignity, and respect.

Gays and Lesbians often fear rejection within their communities. They feel under pressure to hide their orientation in an attempt to "fit in" with supposedly conventional "straight" society

I believe strongly that their families need to support, and if necessary, protect them. Anyone motivated by prejudice, by a hatred or intense dislike of Gays or Lesbians, would do well to remember God's compassionate advice: "Suffer the little children to come unto me ..." We are all equal in the sight of God.

Gays and lesbians will experience no discrimination on the Other Side as they do here. It is only on earth that such hurtful prejudice and narrow-minded bigotry prevails.

But any of us who indulge in hateful or prejudicial behaviour towards these fellow citizens will have to answer for our intolerance.

Such an attitude will impede our spiritual progress and hold us back if we persist in condemning and rejecting people whose only "crime" is to have a different sexual preference.

I urge readers to show tolerance, respect, and understanding towards people who embody or express minority sexual or behavioural dispositions. They are here on earth to learn, and evolve spiritually, like everybody else, and we should bear this in mind.

The same applies to other minorities. There is a lot of racism and blind, unreasoning prejudice in the world. Ireland is not exempt from this disease that infects communities worldwide. We must remember at all times that the colour of one's skin will make no difference to our status on the Other Side.

It's how we behave and what we achieve that counts, and how our actions affect others. God doesn't favour any skin colour or ethnic group over any other, regardless of what misguided notions, philosophies, or ideologies have driven or inspired people to believe otherwise throughout the millennia.

Racial hatred, or unjust discrimination directed against minorities cannot be condoned. Apart from the hurt, whether physical or psychological, inflicted on the victims of racism, the perpetrators will have to answer for their blindness in the afterlife, or in a future life on earth.

From my direct perception of life on the Other Side, I can assure readers that the notion of any one race being superior to another is pure myth and fantasy.

We are all equal in the sight of God. Those of you who suffer the pain of hatred, bigotry, and misunderstanding will find peace, liberty, and healing in the next life.

In-laws or Outlaws:
The Pain of "Outcasting"

ANOTHER ISSUE I find coming up repeatedly in my readings is the painful and almost taboo subject of family break-ups and the life-long hurt they cause to people on all sides of a domestic dispute or dead relationship.

Vast numbers of people walk the streets of this country who cannot, or will not, speak to, or even acknowledge, their own flesh and blood, be they grandparents, uncles, great-grandparents, cousins or other relatives.

Simply because they have mentally rejected and spurned these people they regard as reminders of a previous unhappy relationship or marriage that has ended.

Just because a couple has broken up and each partner gone their separate ways, close family relations and members of the extended families of both partners seem to feel obliged to "go on strike" – permanently, in a kind of misguided "sympathy" with their sides of the splintered family or conjugal partnership.

Not content with just reacting badly to the actual break-up – a natural response to a difficult crossroads in anybody's life – they find it necessary to turn what should be a temporary period of reflection and post-mortem for those directly involved into a LIFE SENTENCE of banishment and exclusion for any relative unlucky enough not to be on THEIR side of the family divide.

I know and have met hundreds of people in the course of my career as a psychic medium who have never known or spoken to grandparents, uncles, aunts, or cousins due to this age-old, extremely hurtful form of ostracism.

They have been warned from childhood not to recognise people who are in fact closely related. They are brought up to believe that they must pass by those people on the street and avoid eye contact with them, pretend to look straight through them.

Family break-ups and the formation of new bonds or relationships are even more common now than in the past. That means even more alienation and more people falling out.

Adults and children regard a break-up from totally different perspectives. An adult who has broken away from a marriage or long term close relationship may see the previous family in extremely negative terms, perhaps with profound hostility, and is relieved to be rid of them.

But the children may have happy memories of the former family arrangement, and of people they are now discouraged from talking to or having any contact with whatsoever.

They feel – and who could blame them? – that they have become victims of a situation that is beyond their control and in which they are given no say. They are hurt at the deepest level by the break-up.

They feel justifiable grief at the loss of people they had come to know and perhaps love; confusion at what is happening in their lives; anger at whomsoever they blame for the situation, and very often a sense of guilt ... if they feel they are somehow partly to blame.

As the weeks turn to months, and the months to years, the children grow up and accept their stepparents or guardians view of their previous family as people to be shunned and not spoken about. They inherit this cruel, selfish, and inhuman attitude that has caused so much hurt and heartache.

Some of the bitterest people who have become embroiled in this unspoken "blood feud" situation; who regard their own in-laws as veritable outlaws, are the very ones you will see licking the altar at Mass, or lecturing others about the finer points of morality and human behaviour.

They cannot see the gulf that separates their high minded ethical standards from the reality of the sadness, trauma, and hurt beyond words that their entrenched, unforgiving attitude has caused.

They cannot grasp that their hostility has a ripple effect, like a pebble tossed into the centre of a lake, that continues long after they have banished their despised relatives from their minds. Many of those relatives turn to drink, drugs, or medication to drown out the bitter memories of lost friendships and acquaintanceship. Others opt to commit suicide.

It has rightly been pointed out by therapists that though a partnership or marriage can be declared officially over and done with, parenthood lasts for life. But this vital consideration is forgotten and brushed aside so quickly, with painful consequences.

Is it not time to end this practise of non-communication between relatives caught up in fractured marriages and relationships? Can we not get around to respecting and acknowledging these "lost ones" in the extended family – our kith and kin – and stop regarding them as throwaways?

For how long more must this terrible charade be maintained, whereby people who may have much in common and could have been the best of friends ARE INSTEAD SEPERATED FOR LIFE BY AN INVISIBLE BARRIER, A WALL OF HATE, MISUNDERSTANDING, REJECTION, AND PERCEIVED GRIEVANCE?

From the Spirit World too I hear the pleading of relatives who passed over without ever knowing their grandchildren or other relatives.

They want to say hello and send love to them. At readings, such people come through to send love and healing to a man or woman who, on earth, never got to know them.

How infinitely sad this is ... and how totally unnecessary!

It is perfectly understandable that ex marriage partners will wish to avoid each other. They have the best reasons to keep a healthy distance, especially if the break-up has been traumatic and painful.

But why on earth should the children of that relationship, and relatives on all sides also have to "divorce" each other and never pass the time of day again?

Lack of forgiveness is at the heart of this crazy but emotionally shattering practise of what I call OUTCASTING. People dig their heels in ... adopt a position of false, immovable, stubborn pride that will not yield.

Perhaps, deep down, they would like to forgive their relatives, but cannot find the courage and the grace to do so. Or maybe they fear the wrath of another family member if they try to break the ice.

That is why I am pleading with anyone out there affected by outcasting who is prepared to listen:

An ability to forgive is a great strength, and situations that require an effort on your part to forgive are central to your progress as a spiritual being on earth.

You are being challenged, every day of the week, in the School of Life.

If you can rise to extending the hand of friendship and forgiveness to those who have hurt or offended you, or against whom you have a grievance (real or imagined), you will be clearing one of those hurdles that are put there to test our degree of spiritual maturity.

Refusing to forgive will set you back, and impede your spiritual advancement.

If you can, please reach out to those forgotten or despised relatives. They will be delighted to hear from you after a long and deathly silence.

I suggest the fixing of a certain date, perhaps in the month of May, as Family Reconciliation Day.

On this day, people could make a special effort to renew old acquaintances, forgive bitter family grievances, and re-establish contact with all those forgotten or un-forgiven relatives who would love to hear from us.

I appeal to voluntary organisations and pressure groups to consider taking up this idea and making it a reality.

Let forgiveness be at the heart of our lives ... and the core theme of Family Reconciliation day.

The Blame Game: The Responsibility is Yours!

THE "BLAME GAME" is one particular habit that has no place on the Other Side. When you arrive on that far shore at the end of life's journey, you must take total responsibility for EVERYTHING, good and bad; that you have ever done on earth. Down here, it is easy and highly convenient to avoid responsibility for one's actions, and for the consequences of those actions.

Communicating spirits confirm time and again that you cannot "get off the hook" of responsibility by blaming someone else for your own mistakes, wrong choices, and misdemeanours.

On earth, we can do it all the time. It is easy to point the finger at someone else in just about every conceivable situation where we cannot face up to the reality of a bad decision, an unwise move, or hurtful behaviour. Denial, accusations, cover-ups, and elaborate smokescreens follow in the wake of people being "found out" or taken to task for almost any form of wrongdoing.

Even if a person is guilty of the most horrific crime, such as murder or sexual abuse, he or she can evade earthly justice by hiring a good lawyer or by committing perjury in court.

In our imperfect world, which is but a poor reflection of the idyllic existence that lies beyond the earth plane, it is possible for evil to achieve temporary success and triumph over good.

Legal systems worldwide are open to corruption and miscarriages of justice. Courts find innocent people guilty and guilty people innocent. Justice and truth are turned on their heads.

We have seen the sneering rapists walking free after getting off on technicalities ... Equally, we have been horrified by cases of men and women who were wrongly convicted of crimes and had their lives ruined.

But even the cleverest wrongdoer cannot escape the light of absolute truth that pervades the Spirit World. The person who slipped through the fingers of lawmakers and enforcers on earth by legalistic subterfuge will not have his high-powered lawyer beside him when he arrives on the Other Side.

He will not be able to press for a dismissal of charges on some obscure "point of law" that will set him free.

He will have to face the Natural Law of the Universe, which is fair and just to everybody. Having reviewed his life, he will see and understand every aspect of his recently terminated earthly lifespan.

He will grasp the enormity of his actions, and appreciate fully, in a way that is difficult to comprehend from this side of the divide, how his life has affected every human being with whom he had any dealings whatsoever on earth.

The rapist will be granted an insight into the pain and suffering he has caused ... The fraudster will see the heartache his trickery has brought to those he duped and defrauded ... the miser will see the lost opportunities his/her stingy attitude has created ...

Likewise the person who falls out with a family member over a silly difference of opinion or perceived affront will appreciate the hurt caused by his/her failure or refusal to make any effort to "mend fences" ... blaming the other person in the dispute is pointless.

Somebody has to make the first move towards reconciliation ... leaving it to the other man or woman is not good enough. WE can break the ice, and not be waiting around for months, years, or decades for Pat or Mary to pick up the phone. It is hard to make the first move ... but think of the relief it will bring to another human being … and think of the value of that kind and thoughtful gesture on your part, not just here on earth, but beyond that, in the life to come.

One does not have to be a blood-crazed, homicidal maniac or sadistic monster to wreak havoc on this planet. A false accusation can destroy a person's life. Betrayal may not be a crime under the law, but it can tear apart the life of even the most level headed or strong-minded human being.

Malicious gossip by just one person can hurt thousands, wreck families, and lead to suicide, a devastated career, or chronic depression. Once the rumour gets out, it grows legs and gallops in all directions and is never short of willing ears to receive and fatten on it.

If the rumour is false and ends up doing harm to a person, the scandalmonger who set the gossip machine in motion will have to take responsibility for that outcome when he/she enters the Spirit World.

There will be no point in saying: "But sure Mary so-and-so or Paddy down the road told more whoppers than I ever did".

Excuses of that kind won't wash "over there". You and you alone will be 'in the dock'. You won't have any solicitor there to argue that you were just a great talker and not really a gossip at all. The truth will be staring you in the face.

You will be granted a vision of all the people you gossiped about … and see the effects of your thoughtless chattering on them.

As I said, the blaming and the denial and the false accusing all come to an end when you reach the great realms of the spirit. Once there, you will not, ever again, be accused in the wrong for the evildoing of others.

But neither will you be permitted to "frame" your fellow men or women for your own shortcomings, failings, crimes, or selfishness. Your sins of commission AND omission will be your own, and you will be free of blame for those committed by any other human being.

When you think about it, this is a much fairer system of justice than the codology we have to put up with down here, where every chancer with a healthy bank balance can run rings around the judges and juries!

In the Spirit World, there is no bribery or corruption ... because there is no money to bribe anyone with. A comedian once joked that all brown envelopes are confiscated at the Gates of Heaven. He wasn't too far off the mark. We have no need of gold or silver or paper currency on the Other Side.

Money exists only on the earth plane, where it has been the root of many evils since the day the first coin was minted. Judas betrayed Jesus for thirty pieces of silver. Politicians today sell their consciences for less. The lack of money feeds poverty and fuels greed.

Though we have no money to spend in the Spirit World, we will be held accountable for how we have used or abused our financial resources down here when we reach the Other Side.

Cutting one's family out of a will can bring untold suffering and bitterness to those who feel cheated by such a heartless decision. Their lack of forgiveness can hold up your progress in the Spirit World.

So, be generous where possible, and spend your money wisely. Remember, one day it will have no value for you but how you decided to spend or invest it may have a huge influence, for good or ill, over the lives of others with whom you share this planet.

CHAPTER 28

Forgiving Their Trespasses

TO ERR is human-to forgive, divine. My work as a medium and psychic counsellor has convinced me of the truth of this age-old maxim.

Though difficult, an ability and willingness to forgive is a fantastic bonus. It enables us to free ourselves from the pain or injustice inflicted on us by others.

It relieves you of the hatred and bitterness-however well deserved-that you may have felt towards the offender, and helps you to put aside harsh judgements and negative thoughts that you will, not surprisingly, have nurtured in the wake of a serious wrong having been perpetrated against you.

Forgiveness is the opposite of condemnation, but it should never be confused with accepting or condoning what your adversary has done to you. You are not just forgiving to benefit the person who wronged you.

You do it to set yourself free from the chains of negative thought patterns that can eat away at your life, affecting you both physically and mentally. You need to forgive in order to enjoy a normal, healthy, happy life.

Despite all the obvious benefits of forgiving, it remains a huge mountain for many of us to climb, depending on the severity of the hurt inflicted on us. It is normal and natural to feel anger against any person who has hurt us: Even more so if he or she has practically ruined our lives.

In readings, I have seen the bitterness and venomous hatred of people who have been wronged ... The very mention of the word forgiveness would have enraged them even further.

The pleadings of spirit relatives who have hurt them in some way fall on deaf ears ... "Never! Never will I forgive you", they repeat. I have heard those words, or similar pain-racked scolding on many occasions.

While understanding, and empathising with, these reactions, I always maintain that it is better in the long run for all concerned to MAKE PEACE.

Letting go of deep-rooted and quite legitimate grievances is never easy. But it is necessary if we are to receive healing, and move on. Very often, a refusal to forgive springs from a need to cling to a "victim mentality", to a need to be pitied and noticed by others.

We cannot live healthy, balanced lives if we allow past wrongs and emotional entanglements to ensnare our present and future situations.

Forgiveness is an antidote to depression, low self-esteem, anxiety, and any number of other soul-destroying effects of retaining, and nurturing, a perpetual sense of victimhood.

We must not allow those dark and possibly nightmarish (in the case of violence or sexual abuse) ordeals from the past continue to overshadow and blight our lives.

Remember that by nursing your grievances, you are allowing yourself to be slowly poisoned by the wrong that you suffered. Who gains from that-you or the other person?

If the person you need to forgive is a partner who betrayed you, you are not excusing his or her behaviour by forgiving them. You are simply ridding yourself of a bitter or vindictive mind-set that the betrayal has provoked in you, and giving yourself a new lease of life, free of negative and ultimately self-destructive thoughts and feelings.

No matter how grievous the wrongdoing, you cannot truly begin to heal the deep hurt caused until you forgive.

We should never think of forgiveness as a sign of weakness. It is the exact opposite. Psychologists will tell you that it is much more powerful than the "power" the bully wields, or the seeming power of anger.

Anyone can be a bully: All it takes is the willingness to tease or torment somebody who seems weaker, or unable to resist. And anger, though it might appear an apt response in many conflict situations, can only bring a temporary release of emotions and frustrations.

But true forgiveness comes from the heart.

The great guides and teachers in the Spirit World deem forgiveness to be one of the highest forms of healing. But it has to be freely given. The choice to forgive must be yours, and yours alone.

It's your decision-whether to remain a prisoner of the past-or to take the courageous step towards the Light of Forgiveness.

LOVE CONQUERS ALL

If you have read about near death experiences, you may have been struck by a common thread that runs through almost all of them, no matter who is involved or what part of the world he or she happens to live.

When the person is revived from "clinical death", you hear a lot about LOVE ... You hear stories of how an advanced spiritual being, enshrouded in light and glowing with compassion, tells the patient whose lifespan has not yet run its course that LOVE IS EVERYTHING.

The actual wording of this simple message may differ from one person to another, but the essential meaning is clear and unambiguous: that love conquers all on this earth ... true love, the unselfish kind that draws people together or motivates acts of great courage or commitment in the service of our fellow human beings.

Love comes from within ... it cannot be bought and sold like a piece of merchandise. It is what enables us to endure and survive life's hardships. I have had my ups and downs, and more than my fair share of hardship ... but the love and the unflinching support of my family got me through.

Love can be shown not only in deeds, but also in thoughts. Remember that thoughts have enormous power ... the potential for great good or monstrous evil. When you think strongly about a person ... in positive or negative terms, you are directing energies in his or her direction.

It is the power of love that comes into play in absent healing. I have helped people over the years who were afflicted by various illnesses. I concentrate on a picture of the one who is ill and send healing to that person.

I may hear afterwards of a change in the person's state of health, or, hopefully, of a marked improvement.

By cultivating the power of love, you can meet and overcome many of the challenges that come your way, dispelling bitterness, hatred, and negativity and replacing these with a force for good that will make life really worth living.

It is better to forgive than to nurse grievances.

Epilogue

I HOPE you have found something of value in this book, whether you have read it through from beginning to end, or just skipped to the chapter headings that caught your attention.

It would take the word power of a vast library of books to even begin to address the many anomalies and mysteries of our evolving, multi-faceted world. And these books would be far beyond one lifetime's reading for even the most ardent bookworm or the most committed student.

But I still like to think that I have opened a little window onto what has been referred to down the ages as "The Great Unknown". Through that small opening may shine a light of revelation.

Readers, I hope, will have caught a glimpse, however brief, doubt-laden, or ephemeral, of the glorious truth that fills the universe and embraces all living beings; the truth that the Big D is not so bad after all, and that in fact it can often be a blessing!

A poet once asked: "Death ... where is thy sting ... or grave thy victory?"

I would answer in the negative to both questions. What we so often regard with horror as the "end" of existence is instead a point of transition to another state of being; a release from pain, illness, or infirmity into lightness, freedom, happiness, youth, and perfect health.

And the grave's dark finality is also an illusion. We should see it, not as the grim location of someone we knew and loved ... but as a fitting memorial to a life that continues elsewhere.

Knowledge of an afterlife takes the sting out of bereavement. It enables one to know, with absolute certainty, that the grave is just an earthly reminder of the transition from one level of existence to another that all of us must make, and that we can all look forward to.

Without moralising or being too "preachy", I hope I have conveyed the importance of living our lives in accordance with the advice: Do unto others what you would have them do unto you.

Unfortunately, this age-old pearl of wisdom has been turned on its head in today's cynical rat-race "Me Fein" era: The priority now has become: Do unto others ... before they can do it to you!

This might seem like a nifty way of freewheeling through the School of Life. But it is utterly at variance with our need to evolve spiritually and overcome the evils that abound on the earth plane.

By respecting the rights, opinions, life styles, and differing psychological make ups of others; we enrich our own lives and store up "credit" in the Bank of Life whose manager is God, the Higher Spirit.

By substituting love for hatred, and dispelling fear with courage, we again supplement our Cosmic Bank Account. People in the Far East call it Karma ... we in the West call it reaping what we sow.

But by whatever name you know it, you can be sure that every good deed will stand to you when the final whistle blows and that referee up the sky signals the end of another game on the pitch of life.

Just as surely, each and every bad or evil deed will have been recorded. So, whatever religion you subscribe to, please ... try to keep out of trouble, at least. Do not kill, injure, character-assassinate, abuse, or betray your fellow men and women. As I emphasise throughout this book, what goes around comes around ... for everybody.

But we should try to go one better than just avoiding the commission of cruel or selfish deeds.

Strive to make the world a better place for those who will inherit it from you, your children and grandchildren, and countless as yet unborn generations of human souls whose future on this planet may depend, in part, on how you live your lives today.

Concentrate on achieving your life mission. In meditation recently, a simple but thought provoking message came to me. I immediately wrote it down: " ... God said ... when your work is done on the earth plane, you come to me for the bonus if you've done your job well ... If you fail to carry out your work, you lose out on the bonus ... "

In other words, we have more to look forward to on the Other Side if we have accomplished our task here. That assignment might be to overcome feelings of jealousy ... or prejudice ... or to care for special needs children ... or to resist the urge to become addicted to something ... or to assist in a national or international war against poverty, injustice, or disease.

It could be a challenge or hurdle revolving around marriage difficulties, or you might have set yourself the task of overcoming personality clashes in work situations and rising above these. From an infinite number of possible life assignments you will have chosen, before birth, one or two that you felt you needed to experience to evolve spiritually.

Whatever your life mission, the rewards are great for attending to it and making your life a success.

When your time comes to leave this earth, you can do so without fear: Goodness, compassion, and the light of perfect understanding will surround you. In the meantime, know that those who passed before you, by whatever means, are in a place that you would not wish to leave if you could call there right now on a momentary visit.

Briefly emerging from a coma before he died, the inventor Thomas Edison uttered his famous last words: "It's beautiful over there". And so it is. I've seen it. I know.

Each one of those dearly departed former inhabitants of Earth has a simple message for you, the one printed on the cover of this book:

Loved Ones ... I'm only a whisper away.